W9-AYF-084

WORLD FLAGS
IDENTIFIER

NORD- UND SÜDAMERIKA

BILD 370-378

Kanada

370 Canadian National Steamships
Montreal

Arbeitsbereich: Montreal–Quebec–Halifax–British
Guinea, Montreal–Vancouver–Südamerika–Austral.
Frachtdampfer: 50
Passagier- und Frachtdampfer: 8
Tonnage ca. 248 180 Regt. brutto

Kanada

371 The Canada Steamship Lines
Montreal

Arbeitsbereich: Große Seen und St. Laurence Strom
Passagier- und Frachtdampfer: 102
Tonnage ca. 308 650 Regt. brutto

Mexico

372 „El Aquila" Compania Mexicana
de Petroleo, Mexico-City

Arbeitsbereich: Mexico–Zentralamerika
Tankdampfer: 5 / Tank-Schleppschiffe: 4
Tonnage ca. 4 850 Regt. brutto

Brasilien

373 Cia de Nav. Lloyd Brazileiro
Rio de Janeiro

Arbeitsbereich: Brasilien–Nordamerika, Europa
Fracht- und Passagierdampf.: 66 / Segler: 1
Motorfrachtschiffe: 4
Tonnage ca. 266 080 Regt. brutto

Brasilien

374 Lloyd Nacional Soc. Anon.
Rio de Janeiro

Arbeitsbereich: Brasilien–Nordamerika
Frachtdampfer: 9 / Tankdampfer: 1
Motor-Passagier- und Frachtschiffe: 4
Tonnage ca. 41 200 Regt. brutto

Argentinien

375 Cia. Argentina de Nav.
(N. Mihanovich Ltda.) Buenos Aires

Arbeitsbereich: Buenos Aires–Südamerika Ostküste
Frachtd.: 25 / Passagierd: 28 / Passagier-Motorsch: 6
Binnensch.: 104 / Schleppsch: 43 / Motorfrachtsch.: 11
Schleppd.: 75 / Motorschleppsch. 7, außerdem versch.
Tankleichter, Vichttransportsch., Schwimmkräne etc.
Tonnage der Passagier-Schi. ca. 50 000 Regt. brutto

Argentinien

376 Sud Atlantica Soc. Anon. de Nav.
Buenos Aires

Arbeitsbereich: Buenos Aires–La Plata, Brasilien
Fracht- und Passagierdampfer: 8
Tonnage ca. 10 000 Regt. brutto

Chile

377 Compania de Vap. Sud-Americana
Valparaiso

Arbeitsbereich: Chile–Peru–Ecuador
Fracht- und Passagierdampfer: 9
Tonnage ca. 31 200 Regt. brutto

Peru

378 Compania Peruana de Vap. y Dique
del Callao, Callao

Arbeitsbereich: Peru–Chile–Ecuador–Nordamerika
Passagier- und Frachtdampfer: 7
Tonnage ca. 29 990 Regt. brutto

ILLUSTRATED ENCYCLOPEDIA

WORLD FLAGS IDENTIFIER

ALFRED ZNAMIEROWSKI

LORENZ BOOKS

This edition is published by Lorenz Books

© 2000, 2001 Anness Publishing Limited

Lorenz Books is an imprint of Anness Publishing Limited
Hermes House, 88-89 Blackfriars Road, London SE1 8HA

Published in the USA by Lorenz Books
Anness Publishing Inc., 27 West 20th Street, New York, NY 10011

www.lorenzbooks.com

Previously published as *Flags of the World,* and as part of a larger compendium, *The World Encyclopedia of Flags*

Publisher: Joanna Lorenz
Project Editor: Helen Marsh
Designer: Michael Morey
Flag artwork: Alfred Znamierowski
Map artwork: Mike Taylor

3 5 7 9 10 8 6 4 2

Author's Acknowledgements

The author wishes to dedicate this book to the memory of his late teacher and friend Dr Ottfried Neubecker,
and to extend thanks for encouragement, help and support to Beata Gierblinska (Warsaw),
Whitney Smith (Winchester, Massachusetts), Roman Klimes (Bonn) and Jacek Skorupski (Warsaw).

Publisher's Acknowledgements

The publisher would like to thank the following for kindly supplying photographs for this book: page 107
tl tm m (3 artworks) Der Flaggenkurier (Achim); page 109 *br* Instytut Wzornictwa Przemyslowego (Warsaw);
page 111 *tr* Alex Majoli and Magnum, *bl* James Nachtwey and Magnum, *br* Robert Van Der Hilst and Tony
Stone Images; page 124 *bl* A. Hornak and Westminster Abbey; page 125 *tr* Bruno Barbey and Magnum.

The publishers would also like to thank: The Flag Design Center, Warsaw for use of images from the archive;
Judy Cox; John Clarke; and Dr Lawrie Wright of Queen Mary and Westfield College, University of London.

Every effort has been made to obtain permission to reproduce copyright material, but there may be cases where we have
been unable to trace a copyright holder. The publisher will be happy to correct any omissions in future printings.

All opinions expressed in this book are those of the author.

◆ HALF TITLE PAGE
The flag of the Nordland Province of Norway.

◆ FRONTISPIECE
Flags of shipping companies of North and South
America in 1933. Plate from *Lloyd Reederei-
Flaggen der Welt-Handelsflotte*, Bremen

◆ TITLE PAGE
National flag of Christmas Island.

◆ OPPOSITE PAGE
National flag and ensign of the Republic of
Zimbabwe, officially introduced in 1980.

◆ THIS PAGE
National flag and ensign of Kazakhstan.

CONTENTS

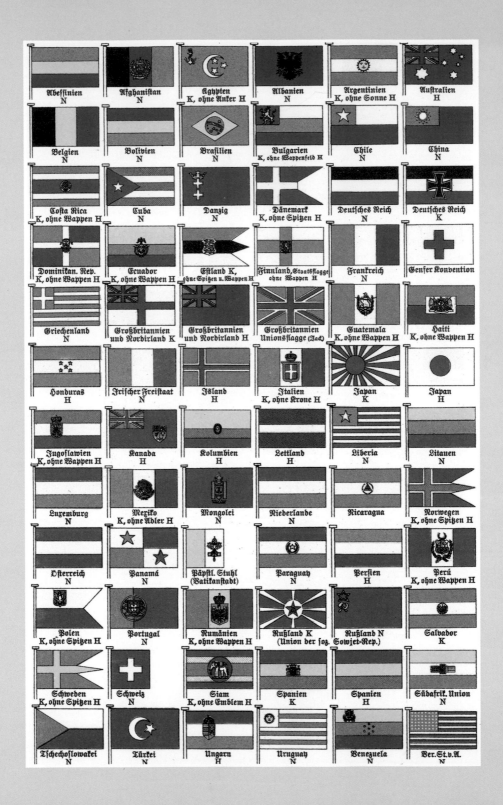

Abessinien N	**Afghanistan** N	**Ägypten** K, ohne Anker H
Albanien	**Argentinien** K, ohne Sonne H	**Australien** H
Belgien N	**Bolivien** N	**Brasilien** N
Bulgarien K, ohne Wappenfeld H	**Chile** N	**China** N
Costa Rica K, ohne Wappen H	**Cuba** N	**Danzig** N
Dänemark K, ohne Spitzen H	**Deutsches Reich** N	**Deutsches Reich** K
Dominikan. Rep. K, ohne Wappen H	**Ecuador** K, ohne Wappen H	**Estland K,** ohne Spitzen u. Wappen H
Finnland, Staatsflagge ohne Wappen H	**Frankreich** N	**Genfer Konvention**
Griechenland N	**Großbritannien und Nordirland** K	**Großbritannien und Nordirland** K
Großbritannien Unionsflagge (Jack)	**Guatemala** K, ohne Wappen H	**Haiti** K, ohne Wappen H
Honduras H	**Irischer Freistaat**	**Island** H
Italien K, ohne Krone H	**Japan** K	**Japan** H
Jugoslawien K, ohne Wappen H	**Kanada** H	**Kolumbien** H
Lettland H	**Liberia** N	**Litauen** N
Luxemburg N	**Mexiko** K, ohne Adler H	**Mongolei** N
Niederlande N	**Nicaragua** N	**Norwegen** K, ohne Spitzen H
Österreich N	**Panamá** N	**Päpstl. Stuhl (Vatikanstadt)**
Paraguay N	**Persien** H	**Perú** K, ohne Wappen H
Polen K, ohne Spitzen H	**Portugal** N	**Rumänien** K, ohne Wappen H
Rußland K (Union der soz. Sowjet-Rep.)	**Rußland N**	**Salvador** K
Schweden K, ohne Spitzen H	**Schweiz** N	**Siam** K, ohne Emblem H
Spanien N	**Spanien** H	**Südafrik. Union** H
Tschechoslowakei N	**Türkei** N	**Ungarn** H
Uruguay N	**Venezuela** N	**Ver.St.v.A.** N

6

Introduction

A thoughtful mind, when it sees a nation's flag, sees not the flag only, but the nation itself; and whatever may be its symbols, its insignia, he reads chiefly in the flag the government, the principles, the truths, the history which belongs to the nation that sets it forth.

HENRY WARD BEECHER (1813–1887), *THE AMERICAN FLAG.*

This comprehensive survey of modern flags is designed to be clear and informative. The national flags of countries of the world are grouped under each continent, with a map of the continent at the beginning to give their location. The word "nation", however, describes not only a state recognized by the international community, but also a community of people of mainly common descent, history, culture, language, and religion who inhabit a territory. So included here are also flags of de facto independent states, autonomous or semi-autonomous territories, and flags of subdivisions of federations and confederations.

Many flags have an interesting story to tell. Even simple colours provide an insight into the symbolic "language" of flags. Some flags show the colours of their natural environment, such as blue for the sea or sky, while in others the colour red may represent the blood spilt by the people in defence of their country. The colours may also refer to an important crop or feature of the landscape, or it may symbolize a virtue or characteristic.

To complete the survey of flags of the world, there are descriptions of regional and local municipal flags used extensively in some countries, and the flags of people and causes. In the 19th and 20th centuries house and private flags became very popular and today there are numerous flags for business, commerce and personal or organizational use, including the high-profile flags of sporting events such as the Olympic Games.

◆ **OPPOSITE**
In 1935 one page was enough to show all the national flags of countries around the world. Today there are four times the number of independent countries. *Courtesy of F.A. Brockhaus GmbH.*

Flags of Europe

In the pages that follow, the current national flags of the countries of Europe, from Iceland and the Faeroes Islands to Russia and Chechnya, and their territories, states and provinces are illustrated and described.

For ease of reference, the countries of Europe have been grouped into geographical areas. We begin with the countries of northern Europe before moving on through central and western Europe and down to south-west Europe, and south and south-east Europe. Finally we look at the flags of the Eastern European countries. There are some geographical anomalies, for example, all Russia's flags are illustrated together in this section. The flags of Turkey, Cyprus and Northern Cyprus are all illustrated here.

For each entry, the country or territory's name is given in its most easily recognized form and then in all its official languages. This is followed by a description of its political status and geographic position. The basic data for each flag contains the status of the flag, date of adoption, proportions, and the symbolic meaning.

ICELAND

Republic of Iceland,
Icelandic **Lýdveldid Ísland.**
Republic comprising an island in the N Atlantic.

CIVIL FLAG AND ENSIGN

*In use since 1913, officially approved 19 June
1915 for use on land and territorial waters, after
1 December 1918 also at sea. Proportions 18:25.
State flag and ensign are swallow-tailed.*

The design of the flag is based on that of
Norway, with the colours reversed. Blue
and white are the traditional national
colours of Iceland and red symbolizes links
with Norway, where most of their ancestors
originated. The Scandinavian cross shows
that Iceland belongs to the family of
Scandinavian countries.

Other symbolic meanings refer to the
natural features of Iceland. Blue is the
colour of the Atlantic Ocean, white
represents the snow and ice covering the
island for most of the year, and red the
volcanoes on the island.

FAEROES ISLANDS

Faeroese **Fóroyar,** Danish **Færøerne.**
Island group in N Atlantic, outlying part of
Denmark with full self-government.

NATIONAL FLAG AND CIVIL ENSIGN

*Introduced in 1919, recognized by the local
parliament in 1931 and officially approved by
the King of Denmark 25 July 1948. The shade of
blue was changed to lighter blue 5 June 1959.
Proportions 8:11.*

The flag was designed by two Faeroese
students in Copenhagen, using Norwegian
and Icelandic colours with the
Scandinavian cross. Red and blue are also
traditional Faeroese colours and the white
represents the foam of the sea and the clear,
bright sky of the Faeroes Islands.

Until 1940 the Faeroese flag was used
only on land but in April 1940, after the
Germans occupied Denmark, Faeroese
ships began to use it at sea. The first to
recognize the Faeroese flag were the British
authorities; it was officially announced in
a BBC broadcast on 25 April 1940 by
Winston Churchill, at that time First Lord
of the Admiralty, and ever since 25 April
has been celebrated as Faeroese Flag Day.

NORWAY

Kingdom of Norway,
Norwegian **Kongeriket Norge.**
Constitutional monarchy in NW Europe.

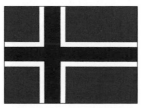

CIVIL FLAG AND ENSIGN

*Adopted 17 July 1821 as a civil ensign only in
N Atlantic, since 1838 usage unrestricted.
Proportions 8:11. Since 1905 state and war flag
and ensign have been triple swallow-tailed.*

From 1748 to 1814 Norwegian ships flew
the Danish *Dannebrog*. In 1814, when
Norway was united with Sweden, the
Norwegians obtained the right to carry the
Dannebrog with the canton charged with
the Norwegian golden lion, crowned and

holding an axe. Nevertheless, the struggle
for a purely Norwegian flag continued and
in 1821 the parliament adopted a new
design, the *Dannebrog* with a dark blue
cross positioned within the white one.
The combination of red, white and blue
followed the French revolutionary *Tricolore*
as well as the flags of the United States and
the United Kingdom, and was at that time
regarded as a symbol of freedom. The cross
was a common symbol of the national flags
of Denmark and Sweden.

DENMARK

Kingdom of Denmark,
Danish **Kongeriget Danmark.**
Constitutional monarchy in NW Europe.

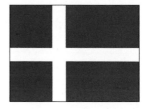

CIVIL FLAG AND ENSIGN

*In use since the 13th century, officially
confirmed in 1625. Proportions 28:37.
State flag and war ensign are swallow-tailed.*

The Danish flag, called the *Dannebrog,* is
probably the oldest national flag in the world.
According to legend, its history begins
when the Danish crusaders, led by King
Valdemar II the Victorious, were
conducting a crusade against the pagan
Estonians. The struggle had been going on
for some time when the Estonians called
all their warriors to arms on St Viti Day,
15 June 1219. The Danes were thrown into
confusion by the fierce and unexpected
attack, but suddenly a sign from heaven,
a great blood red flag with a white cross
floated down from the sky. The retreating
Danish soldiers caught the flag, counter-
attacked with the cry of "Forward to victory
under the sign of the Cross", and eventually
won the battle.

There is no definite proof that the *Dannebrog* was used at such an early date; the first picture of it appeared in *Wapenboek Gelre* in the second half of the 14th century. However, the *Dannebrog* may originally (in the 12th century) have been a crusade banner or even an ensign. The most probable theory is that the *Dannebrog* evolved in the same way as the flags for the border territories of the Holy Roman Empire (Hanseatic cities or cities in northern Italy), most of which displayed a white cross on red or red on white.

SWEDEN

Kingdom of Sweden,
Swedish **Konungariket Sverige**.
Constitutional monarchy in NW Europe.

CIVIL FLAG AND ENSIGN

Introduced in the 16th century, usage regulated on 6 November 1663, the most recent regulations of colours and proportions laid down in the Flag Act of 1982. Proportions 5:8.

In the royal warrant of 1569, King John III decreed that the golden cross should always be borne on Swedish battle banners. The oldest recorded pictures of the blue flag with a yellow cross date from the end of the 16th century, while reliable evidence that it was also the ensign of Swedish vessels dates from the 1620s. According to the oldest existing flag warrant from 1663, a triple-tailed flag was to be used by all except merchant ships, whose ensign was rectangular. Nowadays, use of the triple-tailed flag is reserved for the royal family and armed forces. The design of the flag was influenced by the Danish *Dannebrog*; its colours were from the coat of arms.

The main shield of the Great Arms of Sweden is divided quarterly and charged with the three crowns of Sweden (in the first and fourth quarters) and the lion of the Folkung dynasty (in the second and third quarters). This arrangement, with a golden cross separating four blue fields, was introduced by King Karl VIII Knutsson in 1448, and set the pattern for the flag.

There are very close ties between Sweden and Denmark, so it cannot be a coincidence that the Swedes added the cross to the arms, as the Danes did in the 14th century, and adopted a flag of the same pattern as the Danish *Dannebrog*.

ÅLAND ISLANDS

Finnish **Ahvenanmaa**, Swedish **Åland**.
Autonomous province of Finland comprising an archipelago in the Baltic Sea.

NATIONAL FLAG

Officially adopted 7 April 1954 for use on land only. Proportions 17:26.

The adoption of the Swedish flag charged with an additional red cross reflects the fact that the population of the islands is predominantly of Swedish origin. The colours are those of the arms of the Åland Islands (golden stag in blue field) and the arms of Finland (golden lion in red field).

FINLAND

Republic of Finland,
Finnish **Suomen Tasavalta**,
Swedish **Republiken Finland**.
Republic in N Europe.

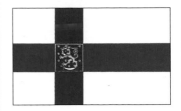

STATE FLAG AND ENSIGN

Adopted 29 May 1918, the most recent regulations came into force 1 June 1978. Proportions 11:18. Civil flag and ensign are without the arms, war ensign is triple swallow-tailed with the arms.

Finland was a part of Sweden from the 12th century until 1809 and, after gaining independence, adopted a national flag patterned on the Swedish one. Similar flags were introduced by Finnish yacht clubs more than half a century earlier, when Finland was under Russian rule. The first yacht club, the *Nyländska Jaktklubben*, was established in 1861 in Helsinki and adopted a white flag with a blue cross, with the arms of the county of Nyland in the canton. The other yacht clubs followed suit, adopting the same design with different arms in the canton. The first to propose the blue and white as national colours of Finland was a poet called Zachris Topelius in 1862. In 1863 the newspaper *Helsingfors Dagblad* suggested that the national flags should be white with a blue cross.

The blue represents the thousands of lakes in Finland and its clear sky; the white stands for the snow that covers the country in the long winters.

ESTONIA

Republic of Estonia, Estonian **Eesti Vabariik**.
Republic in N Europe.

NATIONAL FLAG, CIVIL AND STATE ENSIGN

*Approved 4 July 1920, re-adopted 8 May 1990.
Proportions 7:11.*

The blue-black-white horizontal tricolour was adopted on 29 September 1881 by the Vironia, the Estonian students' association, and was displayed in great numbers at national song festivals in both 1894 and 1896. During the revolutions in 1905 and 1917 it was used by the populace as a national flag, and when independence was proclaimed on 24 February 1918 it became the Estonian civil flag.

In Estonian folk songs the colours of the flag symbolize the sky (blue), the soil (black) and the aspiration to freedom and hope for the future (white). Another interpretation is blue for mutual confidence and fidelity; black for the supposed ancestors of the Estonians, the black-cloaked people mentioned in Herodotus' *Histories*; and white for the snow that covers the country for half the year.

LATVIA

Republic of Latvia.
Latvian **Latvijas Republika**.
Republic in N Europe.

NATIONAL FLAG, CIVIL AND STATE ENSIGN

*Approved 15 June 1921, re-adopted
15 February 1990. Proportions 1:2.*

In 1279, long before it became the national flag of Latvia, the red-white-red banner was used by the home guard of Cesis. It was revived in 1870 by a group of Latvian university students in Estonia and used in 1873 at a national song festival in Riga. During World War I these colours became popular and were used by Latvian units of the Russian army, by boy scouts and by civil organizations. In 1917 prominent Latvian artists agreed that the shade of red should be crimson and that the width of the white stripe should be one-fifth of the flag's width. Use of the flag was forbidden under the Soviet occupation, which started on 17 June 1940. On 29 September 1988 its use as a civil flag was legalized and in 1990 it again became the national flag.

LITHUANIA

Republic of Lithuania,
Lithuanian **Lietuvos Respublika**.
Republic in N Europe.

NATIONAL FLAG, CIVIL AND STATE ENSIGN

*Hoisted 11 November 1918, re-adopted
20 March 1989. Proportions 1:2.*

Since the end of the 14th century the historic flag of Lithuania was red with a white knight and, in 1918, this became the state flag. The Lithuanian Council appointed a special commission to design a national flag and on 19 April 1918 it approved a horizontal tricolour using the colours most popular in traditional Lithuanian cloth.

The yellow is the colour of the sun, symbolizing light, prosperity, nobility, honesty and spiritual greatness. The green is the colour of vegetation, symbolizing the beauty of nature, life, hope, freedom and joy. The red is the colour of the land and of blood, symbolizing love, daring, courage and blood shed for the Fatherland.

THE *VYTIS*

The Lithuanian arms were adopted in the late 14th century. They are called *vytis* in Lithuanian which means "dispatch rider" or "knight". However, since the verb *vyti* means "to pursue, to follow hastily in order to overtake", the name of the arms in English can be translated as "the pursuit".

The Lithuanian arms or "pursuit" depict an armoured medieval knight riding hard on a galloping horse with a sword above his head.

Until the end of the 18th century "the pursuit" appeared on a red field on all Lithuania's battle and state banners. Then,

when Lithuania regained its independence in 1918, the *vytis* or "pursuit" became the main figure on the obverse of both the state and the presidential flag.

The arms were restored again in 1991 and appeared on the presidential standard and military colours.

CENTRAL EUROPE

POLAND

Republic of Poland,
Polish **Rzeczpospolita Polska**.
Republic in central Europe.

CIVIL ENSIGN, STATE FLAG OF LIMITED USE

In use since 1916, approved 1 August 1919.
Proportions 5:8. Civil flag is without arms.

This is the only state flag in the world that is not used by all of the government authorities. According to the law, it may be used only by Polish representations abroad, civil airports and airfields, harbour authorities and civil aircraft abroad.

The Polish arms are over 700 years old and show a white eagle on a red shield. Officially approved in 1831 as the colours of the national cockade, they became popular during World War I.

SLOVAKIA

Slovak Republic,
Slovak **Slovenská Republika**.
Republic in Central Europe.

NATIONAL FLAG

Adopted 1 September 1992. Proportions 2:3.

The first Slovak flag, a horizontal tricolour of white-blue-red, appeared in 1848. The colours are those of the arms (white patriarchal cross, blue triple mountain,

red shield). The same flag was adopted on 23 June 1939 as the national flag of independent Slovakia and remained in use until 1945. It again became official on 1 March 1990 and was used in Slovakia, which at that time was part of Czechoslovakia. The present flag was described in the constitution of 1 September 1992, four months before Slovakia became an independent republic.

CZECH REPUBLIC

Czech **Česká Republika**.
Republic in central Europe.

NATIONAL FLAG

Adopted 20 March 1920 as the flag of Czechoslovakia, proclaimed the flag of the Czech Republic 17 December 1992. Proportions 2:3.

White and red are the traditional colours of Bohemia; they stem from the arms (which feature a white lion on a red field), which date back to 1192. The first Czech white and red bicolour flag appeared during World War I and in 1918 became the first national flag of Czechoslovakia. As it displayed only the colours of Bohemia, the blue from the arms of Moravia and Slovakia was added in 1920.

HUNGARY

Republic of Hungary, Hungarian **Magyar Köztársaság**. Republic in Central Europe.

NATIONAL AND STATE FLAG

Adopted in 1848, re-introduced 1 October 1957.
Proportions 2:3.

The first recorded instance of the Hungarian national colours (red, white, green) dates from a drum cover of the mid-16th century. From the beginning of the 17th century they were used in the seal cord, and later were an important part of the decorations used at coronations. In the 1830s patriotic elements started to use flags with these colours, and during the revolution of 1848 the Hungarian tricolour was proclaimed as the national flag. The colours are those of the Hungarian arms (red shield, white stripes and patriarchal cross, green triple mountain).

AUSTRIA

Republic of Austria,
German **Republik Österreich**.
Federal republic in central Europe.

STATE FLAG

Adopted 1 May 1945. Civil flag and ensign are without arms.

From at least 1230 the Austrian arms consisted of a red shield with a wide

13

horizontal white bar. The red-white-red stripes first appeared on the state and war ensign, introduced on 1 January 1787. The red-white-red horizontal bicolour with no charge was adopted in 1918 as the national flag and in 1921 as the civil ensign. After the German occupation of 1938–1945, the flag was re-introduced in 1945.

AUSTRIAN STATES

Austria is divided into nine states (Bundesländer) which have their own flags.

BURGENLAND

STATE FLAG

Adopted 25 June 1971. Proportions 2:3.

The arms in the centre of the horizontal bicolour of livery colours were introduced in 1922. They combine the arms of two families, the counts of Güssing-Bernstein and the counts of Mattersdorf-Forchtenstein, who had extensive estates in Burgenland before they died out in the 15th century.

CARINTHIA

STATE FLAG

Officially adopted 18 June 1946. Proportions 2:3.

This flag has been in use since the 19th century. The colours stem from the arms, which date back to the 13th century.

They were officially adopted in 1930 as the arms of the province.

LOWER AUSTRIA

STATE FLAG

Officially adopted 9 August 1954.
Proportions 2:3.

The flag was introduced in the 19th century. The colours are those of the arms (five golden eagles on a blue field), adopted in 1359.

SALZBURG

STATE FLAG

Officially adopted 16 February 1921.
Proportions 2:3.

The red-white bicolour has been in use since the 19th century. The colours derive from the second field of the provincial arms and bear the colours of Austria.

STYRIA

STATE FLAG

Officially adopted in 1960. Proportions 2:3.

In the 19th century the flag of Styria was a green-white bicolour; the colours then were reversed in 1960. They are the colours of the arms, which date back to the 13th century and display a silver panther on a green field.

TYROL

STATE FLAG

Officially adopted 10 March 1949.
Proportions 2:3.

A red eagle on a silver (white) field has been the arms of Tyrol since the 13th century. A crown was added in 1416, and a green wreath in 1567. The present form of the arms was introduced in 1946.

UPPER AUSTRIA

STATE FLAG

Officially adopted 25 April 1949.
Proportions 2:3.

The arms date back to the 14th century and were confirmed in 1930. The colours of the flag stem from the second field of the arms (white and red pallets).

VIENNA

STATE FLAG

Approved in 1946. Proportions 2:3.

The red-white flag has been in use since the first half of the 19th century. The colours are those of the arms (white cross on red field).

VORARLBERG

STATE FLAG

Approved in 1946. Proportions 2:3.

Introduced in the 19th century, the flag's colours are those of the provincial arms, based on the arms of the dukes of Montford, which date back to the end of the 12th century (red gonfanon on silver field).

LIECHTENSTEIN

Principality of Liechtenstein,
German **Fürstentum Liechtenstein**.
Constitutional monarchy in W Central Europe.

NATIONAL FLAG

Adopted 24 June 1937, the crown modified 18 September 1982. Proportions 3:5.

The national colours of Liechtenstein probably derive from the blue and red livery used in the 18th century by the servants of Prince Joseph Wenzel of Liechtenstein. The horizontal bicolour was confirmed as the national flag in the constitution signed on 5 October 1921. In 1937 the prince's crown was introduced to distinguish it from the civil flag of Haiti.

SWITZERLAND

Swiss Confederation,
German **Schweizerische Eidgenossenschaft,**
French **Confédération Suisse,**
Italian **Confederazione Svizzera,**
Romansch **Confederaziun Svizra**.
Federal republic in W Central Europe.

NATIONAL FLAG

Officially adopted 12 December 1889. Proportions 1:1. Proportions of civil ensign 2:3.

In 1339 every soldier and officer of the troops leaving for the battle of Laupen was marked with the sign of the Holy Cross. The white cross on a red field has been a common Swiss emblem ever since. From the end of the 15th century a red banner charged with a white cross has been the accepted flag of the Confederation. The current flag was introduced in 1848 as the military colours, and its exact proportions were established in a military regulation of 1852. It became the national flag in 1889.

SWISS CANTONS

The official flags of all Swiss cantons are square armorial banners (*Kantonsfahnen*). Other types of Swiss flags are: (i) a long, vertical, swallow-tailed banner with a square armorial flag in the hoist and vertical stripes in livery colours (*Wappenflagge*); (ii) a long, vertical, rectangular banner of the same design as above, hanging from a traverse projecting at a right angle from a mast (*Knatterfahne*); (iii) a long, vertical, swallow-tailed banner in livery colours (*zweizipflige Farbenfahne*); (iv) a rectangular flag of proportions 2:3 in livery colours (*querrechteckige Farbenfahne*).

AARGAU

CANTONAL FLAG

Adopted in 1803, present form since 1930.

The white waves symbolize the River Aare, and the stars stand for the districts of Baden, Freien Ämter and Fricktal. The livery colours are black and blue.

APPENZELL INNER-RHODES

CANTONAL FLAG

In use since the beginning of the 15th century.

The bear was taken from the arms of the Abbey of Sankt Gallen. The livery colours are white and black.

APPENZELL OUTER-RHODES

CANTONAL FLAG

Adopted in 1597.

When the canton separated from Appenzell, the bear was retained and the letters "VR" (the initial letters for Ussroden – Outer-Rhodes) were added. The livery colours are white and black.

BASEL-LAND

CANTONAL FLAG

Introduced in 1834, the present form established 1 April 1947.

The arms are based on the civic arms of Liestal. The livery colours are white and red.

BASEL-STADT

CANTONAL FLAG

In use since at least the 15th century.

The oldest known representation of the bishop's crozier is on a coin minted in the 11th century; the current shape of the crozier has been in use since the 13th century. The livery colours are white and black.

BERN

CANTONAL FLAG

In use since at least the 14th century.

These are canting arms, i.e. they contain an allusion to the name of the canton (the German word for "bear" is *Bär*). The oldest representation of the bear is on a coin minted in 1224. The livery colours are red and black.

FRIBOURG

CANTONAL FLAG

In use since the beginning of the 15th century.

The arms, based on the banner, were adopted in 1477. The livery colours are black and white.

GENEVA

CANTONAL FLAG

In use since the 15th century.

The black eagle is the emblem of the Holy Roman Empire and the key is a symbol of St Peter. The oldest representations of the arms are in two books published in 1451. The livery colours are yellow and red.

GLARUS

CANTONAL FLAG

In use since the 14th century. The present form adopted 25 June 1959.

The patron saint of the canton is St Fridolin, an Irish missionary who settled there in 500. The livery colours are black, white and red. The black and white together are the same width as a red stripe.

GRAUBÜNDEN

CANTONAL FLAG

Adopted 8 November 1932.

The arms display the symbols of the three parts of the canton, which united in the 15th century: *Grauer Bund* (black and white), *Zehgerichtenbund* (cross) and *Gotteshausbund* (ibex). The livery colours are black, white and blue.

JURA

CANTONAL FLAG

Adopted in 1951, approved in 1976, official since 1978.

The crozier recalls that Jura was part of Basel-Land. The stripes represent seven districts interested in being part of a new canton. In the end only three formed Jura. The livery colours are white and red.

LUCERNE

CANTONAL FLAG

In use since the 13th century.

The canton's colours are older than the arms (adopted in 1386). In the arms the colours are arranged vertically: blue, white. The livery colours are white and blue.

NEUCHÂTEL

CANTONAL FLAG

Adopted 11 April 1848.

The green represents liberty, the white and red are traditional Swiss colours. The livery colours are green, white and red.

NIDWALDEN

CANTONAL FLAG

In use since the beginning of the 15th century.

The key is the emblem of St Peter. The livery colours are red and white.

OBWALDEN

CANTONAL FLAG

Adopted 12 August 1816.

Since the 13th century the canton's arms and banner have been a red-white bicolour. The key of St Peter appeared for the first time on the seal in the 13th century. The livery colours are red and white.

SAINT GALL

CANTONAL FLAG

Adopted 4 April 1803.

The fasces is a symbol of sovereignty and unity; the eight rods (five are visible) represent the eight districts of the canton. The livery colours are green and white.

SCHAFFHAUSEN

CANTONAL FLAG

In use since the 14th century.

The ram (*Schafsbock* in German) alludes to the name of both the city and the canton. Since the 15th century the canton's colours have been green and black.

SCHWYZ

CANTONAL FLAG

In use since the 15th century.

Since the end of the 13th century the banner has been plain red. The oldest recorded picture of a banner with a white cross in the canton dates from 1470. The livery colour is red. The white cross appears on the *zweizipflige Farbenfahne*.

SOLOTHURN

CANTONAL FLAG

In use since the 14th century.

The livery colours are red and white.

THURGAU

CANTONAL FLAG

Adopted 13 April 1803.

The lions are from the arms of the counts of Kyburg. Green represents freedom. The livery colours are green and white.

TICINO

CANTONAL FLAG

Adopted 23 May 1803.

The colours (vertical in the arms, horizontal on the banner) were established in 1930. The livery colours are red and blue.

URI

CANTONAL FLAG

In use since the 14th century.

From the 13th to the 15th century the aurochs's head was without the nose-ring. The emblem (*Uroch* in Old German) alludes to the name of the canton. The livery colours are yellow and black.

VALAIS

CANTONAL FLAG

In use since the 16th century, present form adopted 12 May 1815.

The stars represent the 13 districts of the canton. The livery colours are white and red.

VAUD

CANTONAL FLAG

Decreed 16 April 1803.

The motto is "Freedom and Fatherland" and the green is a symbol of freedom. The livery colours are white and green.

ZUG

CANTONAL FLAG

In use since the mid-14th century.

The arms and banner were originally identical to those of Austria (red field with white band) and were changed when Zug joined the Confederation in 1352. The livery colours are white, blue and white.

ZÜRICH

CANTONAL FLAG

In use since the 13th century.

The oldest known representation of the arms dates from 1389. The livery colours are blue and white.

GERMANY

Federal Republic of Germany, German **Bundesrepublik Deutschland**. Federal republic in Central Europe.

STATE FLAG

Introduced 23 March 1848, re-introduced in 1919 and again 23 May 1949. Civil flag and ensign are without arms.

The German national colours are those of the arms, which are the same as the arms of the Holy Roman Empire: black for the eagle, red for its beak and claws, and yellow for the golden shield. They featured in the uniform worn by the Lützow Free Corps (black greatcoats, red facings and liems, golden buttons) during the war of liberation in 1813–1815, when the trend towards the unification of Germany was growing. The horizontal tricolour of black-red-gold became the national flag of the German Federation in 1848 and was replaced in 1867 with a tricolour of black-white-red, which was in use until 1919 and again in 1933–1935.

GERMAN STATES

From 1949 to 1990 West Germany comprised 11 states (Bundesländer). Since re-unification with East Germany there are now 16 states.

BADEN-WÜRTTEMBERG

STATE FLAG

Adopted 29 September 1954. Proportions 3:5.

Black and yellow have been the colours of the arms of the duchy of Swabia since the end of the 12th century. They display three black lions on a golden shield.

BAVARIA

STATE AND CIVIL FLAG

Adopted 2 December 1946. Proportions 3:5.

The Bavarian flag is a horizontal bicolour in the livery colours. The arms of Bavaria, which date back to the beginning of the 13th century, have white and blue lozenges.

BERLIN

STATE FLAG

Adopted 13 May 1954. Proportions 3:5.

The bear first appeared on the second city seal in 1280. A red-white-red flag with a black bear was introduced in 1913, and the current design of the bear was established in 1954.

CIVIL FLAG

BRANDENBURG

STATE AND CIVIL FLAG

Adopted 30 January 1991. Proportions 3:5.

The arms date back to 1330. The flag is in the livery colours.

BREMEN

STATE AND CIVIL FLAG

In use without arms since 1691, approved 21 November 1947. Proportions 2:3.

The originally plain red flag was charged in the second half of the 14th century with a white key, the symbol of St Peter, the patron saint of the city. The current forms of the great and small arms, and two state flags, were enacted in 1891.

HAMBURG

STATE FLAG

Civil flag adopted 14 May 1751, state flag introduced 8 October 1897, confirmed 6 June 1952. Proportions 2:3.

CIVIL FLAG

The castle represents Hammaburg Castle, built by Emperor Charles the Great in AD 808, and the arms date back to 1254. The three towers stand for the Trinity, the cross is a symbol of Christ, and the stars symbolize God the Father and the Holy Spirit. Red flags with the castle were already in use in the first half of the 14th century.

HESSE

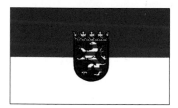

STATE AND CIVIL FLAG

Both flags adopted 22 November 1949. Proportions 3:5.

The colours of the flag are taken from the lion in the arms. These stem from the arms of the landgraves (ruling counts) of Thuringia, who from 1130 to 1247 were also landgraves of Hesse.

LOWER SAXONY

CIVIL FLAG

Adopted 13 April 1951. State flag is swallow-tailed. Proportions 2:3.

The flag is in the German national colours and is charged with the arms of the state. The horse (*Niedersachsenross*) has been the symbol of Lower Saxony since the 14th century.

MECKLENBURG-WEST POMERANIA

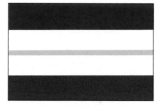

CIVIL FLAG

Adopted 29 January 1991. Proportions ±3:5.

The flag is a combination of the colours of Pomerania (blue, white), Hansa (white, red) and former flags of Mecklenburg – the national flag (blue, yellow, red) and the civil ensign (blue, white, red).

NORTH RHINE-WESTPHALIA

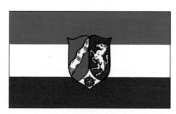

STATE FLAG

Adopted 10 March 1953. Civil flag is without arms. Proportions 3:5.

The colours of the flag are taken from the arms, which combine the symbols of three parts of the state which are Rhineland (river), Westphalia (horse) and Lippe (rose).

RHINELAND-PALATINATE

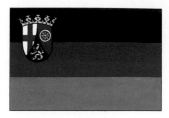

STATE AND CIVIL FLAG

Adopted 10 May 1948. Proportions 2:3.

The flag is in the colours of Germany and the state arms. The arms combine the arms of Trier (cross), Koblenz (wheel) and Palatinate (lion), all dating back to the 13th century.

SAARLAND

STATE AND CIVIL FLAG

Adopted 9 July 1956, introduced 1 January 1957. Proportions ±3:5.

This is the national flag of Germany with the state arms. The arms are quarterly: (i) countship of Saarbrücken, (ii) Trier, (iii) Lorraine, (iv) Palatinate.

SAXONY

STATE FLAG

Adopted 16 June 1815. Civil flag is without arms. Proportions 3:5.

The civil flag, used 1815–1935 and 1947–1952, was re-adopted in 1991. The arms are those of the duchy of Saxony and date back to the 13th century.

SAXONY-ANHALT

STATE FLAG

Civil flag (without arms) adopted 29 January 1991. State flag described in the constitution of 1992. Proportions 3:5.

The black and yellow bicolour was the flag of the Prussian province of Saxony from 1884–1935 and 1945–1952. The order of the colours has been reversed to differentiate the flag from that of Baden-Württemberg. The arms used are a combination of the arms of Saxony (black and yellow bands, green crown of rue), Anhalt (black bear on red wall) and Prussia (black eagle).

SCHLESWIG-HOLSTEIN

STATE FLAG

Adopted 18 January 1957. Civil flag is without the arms. Proportions 3:5.

The blue-white-red horizontal tricolour became the civil flag for use on land in 1842. This flag was used until 1854, and again in 1864–1935. The colours were taken from the arms, which depict the blue lions of Schleswig and the white nettle leaf of Holstein.

THURINGIA

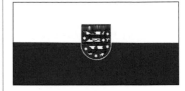

STATE FLAG

Adopted 10 January 1991. Civil flag is without the arms. Proportions 1:2.

The flag shows the colours of the Thuringian white and red lion, dating from the 12th century. The white stars were added to the arms to commemorate the seven small states that formed the province of Thuringia in 1920.

WESTERN EUROPE

LUXEMBOURG

Grand Duchy of Luxembourg,
French **Grand-Duché de Luxembourg,**
Letzeburgesch **Groussherzogtum Lëtzebuerg,**
German **Grossherzogtum Luxemburg.**
Constitutional monarchy in W Europe.

NATIONAL FLAG

Introduced in the present form 12 June 1845, adopted 16 August 1972. Proportions 3:5.

It is only coincidence that this flag is so similar to that of the Netherlands. The colours of the national flag of Luxembourg are those of the arms (red lion, white and blue stripes). Note the lighter shade of blue. An armorial banner has been in use since 1853 as the flag of the Army, and since 1972 as the flag of inland shipping and civil aviation.

FRANCE

Republic of France,
French **République Française.**
Republic in W Europe.

NATIONAL FLAG

Introduced 20 May 1794, uninterrupted use since 5 March 1848.
Proportions 2:3. Civil and war ensign have stripes of different width.

The colours of the French national flag, known as the *Tricolore*, were introduced during the French Revolution when the King added the royal white cockade of the House of Bourbon to the revolutionary cockade of blue and red (the livery colours of Paris).

BELGIUM

Kingdom of Belgium, Flemish **Koninkrijk België**, Walloon **Royaume de Belgique**. Federal constitutional monarchy in W Europe.

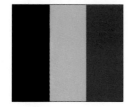

NATIONAL FLAG

Introduced August 1830, officially adopted 23 January 1831. Proportions 13:15, proportions of civil ensign 2:3.

The flag, inspired by the French *Tricolore*, displays the colours of the arms of the duchy of Brabant, which date back to the 12th century. The war of independence started in Brabant and found its greatest support there, so its arms became the arms of Belgium (golden lion with red claws and tongue on black field).

BELGIAN REGIONS

In 1993 Belgium became a federal state comprising three nearly autonomous regions: Flanders (Flemish-speaking), Wallonia (French-speaking), and Brussels (bilingual). Each has its own parliament, regional council and government.

BRUSSELS

REGIONAL FLAG

Adopted on 22 June 1991. Proportions ±2:3.

The blue is that of the flag of the European Union. The iris is a well-known flower of the fields along the river Senne which flows through Brussels.

FLANDERS

REGIONAL FLAG

Introduced 11 July 1985. Proportions 2:3.

This is an armorial flag, the basic design of which dates from the 12th century.

WALLONIA

REGIONAL FLAG

Introduced in 1913. Proportions 2:3.

The cock is a traditional Gallic emblem and recalls Wallonia's linguistic and cultural ties with France.

THE NETHERLANDS

Kingdom of the Netherlands, Dutch **Koninkrijk der Nederlanden**. Semi-federal constitutional monarchy in W Europe.

NATIONAL FLAG AND ENSIGN

Officially introduced 14 February 1796, confirmed 19 February 1937. Proportions 2:3.

The first flag of the Netherlands, introduced in 1574 during the struggle for independence, was a horizontal tricolour of orange-white-blue. Orange was the colour of William I, Prince of Orange, who led the rebellion against Spanish rule and eventually in 1581 established an independent country. During the 17th century red gradually replaced the orange, and in 1796 the red-white-blue was officially confirmed.

Nevertheless, orange is still the Dutch national colour and when the flag is displayed during state holidays or by diplomatic missions abroad it is accompanied by a long orange streamer fastened just above the flag.

THE NETHERLANDS PROVINCES

While all Dutch port cities had their own flags already in the 17th century, the provincial flags came into being during the last 50 years. Nevertheless, they display livery colours or arms that are several centuries old.

DRENTHE

PROVINCIAL FLAG

Adopted 19 February 1947. Proportions 9:13.

White and red are the colours of the bishopric of Utrecht, to which the province once belonged. The black castle is the castle of Coevorden, where in 1227 the rebellion against the bishopric started. The stars represent the former six *fehmic* courts.

FLEVOLAND

PROVINCIAL FLAG

Adopted 9 January 1986. Proportions 2:3.

The flag recalls how the new province was reclaimed from the waters of the IJsselmeer. The dark yellow central stripe, wavy then straight, symbolizes the transformation of the sea into land. Its colour is that of rape, planted in the new polders to stabilize the land; the blue represents water, the green the land. The fleur-de-lis honours C. Lely, who designed the original polders.

FRIESLAND

PROVINCIAL FLAG

Adopted 9 July 1957. Proportions 9:13.

The design is based on the arms from the 15th century. The stripes and waterlily leaves represent the districts of Friesland.

GELDERLAND

PROVINCIAL FLAG

Adopted 13 April 1953. Proportions 9:13.

The colours are those of the provincial arms, combining the arms of the old dukedoms of Gelre (golden lion in blue field) and Gulik (black lion in golden field).

GRONINGEN

PROVINCIAL FLAG

Adopted 17 February 1950. Proportions 2:3.

Green and white are Groningen's colours; red, white and blue are Ommerland's.

LIMBURG

PROVINCIAL FLAG

Adopted 28 July 1953. Proportions 2:3.

The blue stripe stands for the river Meuse and the lion comes from the arms of the duchy of Limburg. Yellow and red are the colours of the arms of Valkenburg, Gulik, Horn and Gelre.

NORTH BRABANT

PROVINCIAL FLAG

Adopted 21 January 1959. Proportions 2:3.

This is the flag of the duchy of Brabant and dates back to the 17th century.

NORTH HOLLAND

PROVINCIAL FLAG

Adopted 22 October 1958. Proportions 2:3.

The colours stem from the arms of Holland (red lion in golden field) and West Friesland (golden lions in blue field).

OVERIJSSEL

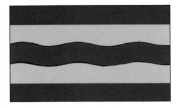

PROVINCIAL FLAG

Adopted 21 July 1948. Proportions 10:17.

The wavy blue stripe symbolizes the river IJssel. The colours are those of the arms (red lion in golden field charged with a blue fesse wavy). They also recall the historic association of the province with Holland.

SOUTH HOLLAND

PROVINCIAL FLAG

Adopted 1 January 1986. Proportions 2:3.

This is the armorial banner of the former countship of Holland.

UTRECHT

PROVINCIAL FLAG

Adopted 15 January 1952. Proportions 2:3.

White and red are the colours of the city of Utrecht. The white cross in a red field is the arms of the bishopric of Utrecht and dates back to the 16th century.

ZEELAND

PROVINCIAL FLAG

Adopted 14 January 1949. Proportions 2:3.

The wavy blue and white stripes symbolize the stripes of sea and land in the coastal area. The arms in the centre date back to the 16th century.

IRELAND

Republic of Ireland,
Irish **Poblacht Na h'Éireann**.
Republic comprising most of the territory of the island of Ireland, NW Europe.

NATIONAL FLAG AND ENSIGN

In use since 1916, recognized in 1922, formally confirmed 29 December 1937. Proportions 1:2.

The flag is based on the French *Tricolore* and displays colours that were used in reverse order during the revolutionary year of 1848. The green represents the Catholics, the orange the Protestants (originally supporters of William of Orange) and the white stands for peace between both parts of the population.

ISLE OF MAN

Isle of Man, Manx **Ellan Vannin**.
Dependency of the British crown in the Irish Sea, NW Europe.

NATIONAL FLAG

Introduced in 1929, present design adopted 9 July 1968. Proportions 1:2.

The distinctive "Three Legs of Man" have been the emblem of the island since at least the 13th century. At the end of the 14th century they were armed and in this form were the main charge of the Manx flags and ensigns.

UNITED KINGDOM

United Kingdom of Great Britain and Northern Ireland.
Constitutional monarchy in NW Europe.

STATE FLAG AND JACK

Adopted 1 January 1801. Proportions 1:2.

The Union flag, also called the Union Jack, is a combination of the crosses of the patron saints of England (St George's cross, red cross on white field), Scotland (St Andrew's cross, white saltire on blue field) and Ireland (St Patrick's cross, red saltire on white field).

UNITED KINGDOM TERRITORIES

Presented here are the flags of the four parts of the United Kingdom (England, Scotland, Wales and Northern Ireland), as

TRISKELION

The *triskelion* (from the Greek for "three-legged") is one of the oldest symbols known to mankind. The earliest representations of it were found in prehistoric rock carvings in northern Italy. It also appears on Greek vases and coins from the 6th and 8th centuries BC, and was revered by Norse and Sicilian peoples. The Sicilian version has a representation of the head of Medusa in the centre.

The Manx people believe that the *triskelion* came from Scandinavia. According to Norse mythology, the *triskelion* was a symbol of the movement of the sun through the heavens.

well as flags of three areas within Scotland that enjoy a limited autonomy (Orkneys, Shetland and the Hebrides).

ENGLAND

NATIONAL FLAG

In use since the 13th century. Proportions ±2:3.

The red cross of St George on a white field was an emblem of the English Army and (until 1606) an ensign of merchant and naval ships. From 1606 to 1801 it was a jack of merchant ships. According to legend, St George saved a princess from a dragon and with its blood made the sign of the cross on his white shield.

SCOTLAND

NATIONAL FLAG

In use since the 12th century. Proportions ±2:3.

St Andrew, brother of St Peter, was a missionary in the area around the Black Sea. He was crucified in Patras on an X-shaped cross, and legend says that some of his relics were taken to Scotland and buried there. Since the 11th century St Andrew has been the patron saint of Scotland, and since the 12th century a white saltire of St Andrew has been the Scottish national symbol (since the 15th century on a blue field).

ORKNEY ISLANDS

NATIONAL FLAG

Introduced in 1975. Proportions 2:3.

In this banner of arms, granted on 3 March 1975, the boat (a traditional galley) is taken from the arms of the countship of the Orkneys. The arms of Norway (a lion holding an axe) recall that the Orkneys originally belonged to Norway and were one of two provinces entitled to use the royal arms.

SHETLAND ISLANDS

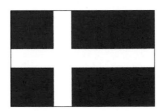

NATIONAL FLAG

In use since 1969. Proportions 2:3.

White and blue are the colours of Scotland. The Scandinavian cross is a reminder that the Shetlands were once settled by the Vikings and indicates that the islands are part of the Nordic countries.

HEBRIDES

NATIONAL FLAG

Granted 9 September 1976. Proportions 1:2.

The British blue ensign is charged with a badge depicting a lymphad (traditional rowing boat) in black. The heraldic boat symbolizes the seafaring traditions and skills of the population.

WALES

NATIONAL FLAG

Approved in 1959. Proportions 2:3.

The red dragon (*Y Ddraig Goch*) dates from the 4th century. In the 7th century it was adopted by Cadwaladr, Prince of Gwynedd, as the charge of his battle standard. White and green were the livery colours of the Welsh Prince Llewellyn, and later of the House of Tudor.

NORTHERN IRELAND

NATIONAL FLAG

Adopted 29 May 1953. Proportions 2:3.

The banner of arms of Northern Ireland was granted by King George V on 2 August 1924. The star representing the six counties is ensigned with the royal crown and charged with the red hand of Ulster. There is a flag of the same design, with a yellow field instead of white.

JERSEY

Bailiwick of Jersey.
Dependency of the British crown in the
English Channel, NW Europe.

NATIONAL FLAG

*Granted by royal warrant of 10 December 1980,
introduced 7 April 1981. Proportions unspecified.*

For about 200 years the flag of Jersey was
white with a red saltire. The arms, added in
1980, are those granted about 1290 by
Edward I, King of England, to the Bailiff of
Jersey. The shield is ensigned with an
ancient crown, similar to that attributed to
the House of Plantagenet.

GUERNSEY

Bailiwick of Guernsey and Dependencies.
Dependency of the British crown in the
English Channel, NW Europe.

NATIONAL FLAG

*Adopted 13 March 1985, officially hoisted
9 May 1985. Proportions 2:3.*

The St George's cross symbolizes
constitutional ties with the British crown,
and the yellow cross of William the
Conqueror recalls that Guernsey was once
part of Normandy. William's banner with
this cross appears several times in the
Bayeaux Tapestry, made in the 11th century.

THE DEPENDENCIES OF GUERNSEY

The Bailiwick of Guernsey comprises
Guernsey, Alderney, Great and Little
Sark, Herm, Brechou, Jethou and
Lihou. Some of the dependencies
have their own flags which are white
with the cross of St George and some
additional devices. The flag of Alderney
(proportions 1:2) has a badge of the
island in the centre. The badge is a
British lion with three leaves in his right
paw on a green disc, framed with a
yellow ornamental border. The flag of
Sark (proportions 1:2) displays two
yellow lions in the red canton. The
canton of the flag of Herm (proportions
3:5) is the banner of arms which
features three monks and two dolphins.
The flag of Leonard Joseph Matchan,
the owner of Brechou (proportions 1:2)
is like that of Sark but has his personal
arms in the lower fly.

SOUTH-WEST EUROPE

PORTUGAL

Republic of Portugal,
Portuguese **República Portuguesa**.
Republic in SW Europe.

NATIONAL FLAG AND ENSIGN

Adopted 19 June 1911. Proportions 2:3.

The red stands for revolution, the green for
hope. The armillary sphere (a navigational
instrument of the Age of Discovery)
commemorates Prince Henry the
Navigator, who inspired the sea voyages
that led to the discovery of new lands and
created Portugal's colonial empire.

The central part of the shield shows the
arms of Portugal, adopted by Alfonso
Henriques after the Battle of Ourique in
1139. The five blue shields represent the
defeated Moorish kings of Lisbon, Badajoz,
Beja, Elvas and Évora. The divine assistance
that enabled Henriques to be victorious is
commemorated on each shield by white
dots representing the five wounds of Christ.

The red border which is charged with
seven yellow castles was added to the arms
after the annexation of Algarve and the
wedding of King Alfonso III and Beatriz
of Castile in 1252.

AZORES

Portuguese **Região Autónoma dos Açores**.
Group of islands in N Atlantic, autonomous
region of Portugal.

NATIONAL FLAG

Adopted 10 April 1979. Proportions 2:3.

The colours of the flag are those of the flag
of Portugal from 1830 to 1911; in the
canton is a shield with the arms of Portugal.
The goshawk (*açor* in Portuguese) refers to

the name of the islands. The nine stars represent the islands of Flores, Corvo, Terceira, São Jorge, Pico, Faial, Graciosa, São Miguel and Santa Maria.

MADEIRA

Portuguese **Região Autónoma da Madeira**.
Island group in E Atlantic, autonomous region of Portugal.

NATIONAL FLAG

Adopted 28 July 1978. Proportions 2:3.

The blue represents the sea, the yellow stands for the land. The cross of the Order of Christ is a reference to Prince Henry the Navigator, who colonized the uninhabited islands.

GIBRALTAR

British dependency in SW Europe.

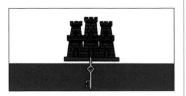

NATIONAL FLAG

Introduced in 1966. Proportions 1:2.

This banner of arms was granted on 10 July 1502 by King Ferdinand and Queen Isabella of Spain, and was confirmed by the British authorities in June 1936. The castle and the key symbolize the strategic importance of the Gibraltar fortress as the key to the Mediterranean.

SPAIN

Kingdom of Spain, Spanish **Reino de España**.
Constitutional monarchy in SW Europe.

STATE FLAG AND ENSIGN

Adopted 28 October 1981. Proportions 2:3.
Civil flag is without arms.

The basic design of the flag (the yellow stripe is twice as wide as each of the red) was introduced on 28 May 1785. With the state arms placed near the hoist, it was until 1931 the war ensign. Without the arms, it was the merchant flag from 1 January 1928 to 27 April 1931. On 29 August 1936 General Franco decreed that it should be the flag and civil ensign of Spain. Since then the state flag is always with the arms, which changed in 1938, 1945, 1977 and 1981.

The colours of the flag are the livery colours of the oldest Spanish kingdoms: the red of León and both colours of Castile, Aragón and Navarre.

SPANISH AUTONOMOUS COMMUNITIES

In 1977–1982 Spain was divided into 17 autonomous communities. They were formed on an ethnic and/or historic basis.

ANDALUSIA

COMMUNITY FLAG

Adopted 30 December 1981. Proportions 2:3.

The colour white represents the homes, the green represents the land.

ARAGÓN

COMMUNITY FLAG

Adopted 14 October 1981. Proportions 2:3.

The armorial banner of Aragón dates from the 14th century. The regional arms display the emblem of the legendary kingdom of Sobrarbe, the white cross of Iñigo Arista, the proper arms of Aragón as used in the 14th century, and the proper arms of Aragón.

ASTURIAS

COMMUNITY FLAG

Adopted 30 December 1981. Proportions 2:3.

The traditional Asturian emblem is the Cross of Victory. From it hang the Greek letters "alpha" and "omega", symbolizing Christ as the Beginning and the End. Blue is the colour of the Virgin Mary.

BALEARES

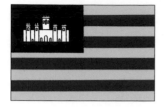

COMMUNITY FLAG

Adopted 25 February 1983. Proportions 2:3.

The flag closely resembles the flag of the kingdom of Mallorca, adopted in 1312. The stripes denote that Baleares has belonged to Aragón since 1228. The castle in the canton is that of Almoraima.

BASQUE COUNTRY

COMMUNITY FLAG

In use since 1894, officially approved 18 December 1979. Proportions 14:25.

The white cross is a symbol of the Catholic faith, the green saltire stands for the holy oak of Guernica and the red field commemorates the blood shed in the struggle for independence. The flag, called *Ikkurina*, was illegal from 1936 to 1977. Persecution for displaying it in public ended on 21 September 1976 and on 19 January 1977 the flag was legalized.

CANARY ISLANDS

COMMUNITY FLAG

Adopted 10 April 1989. Proportions 2:3.

The white represents the snow covering the volcano Pico de Teide on the island of Tenerife, the blue stands for the sea and the yellow for the sun.

CANTABRIA

COMMUNITY FLAG

Adopted 30 December 1981. Proportions 2:3.

White and red are the traditional colours of the region.

CASTILLA-LA MANCHA

COMMUNITY FLAG

Adopted 30 June 1983.
Proportions 1:2, actual flags differ.

This banner of arms displays the arms of Castile in the hoist and in the fly the colour of the surcoats worn by the crusaders.

CASTILLA-LEÓN

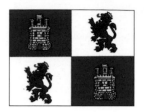

COMMUNITY FLAG

Adopted 25 February 1983. Proportions 76:99.

This regional armorial banner is the same as that used by Spain from 1230 to 1479. It displays canting arms referring to Castile (castle) and León (lion).

CATALONIA

COMMUNITY FLAG

In use since the 13th century, confirmed in 1932. Proportions 2:3.

The flag displays the stripes of the medieval arms of Catalonia (four red pallets on a golden field), arranged horizontally. Use of this flag was illegal from 1939 to 1975.

EXTREMADURA

COMMUNITY FLAG

Adopted 3 June 1985. Proportions 2:3.

The colours of the flag are those of the two parts of the region, Cáceres (green and white) and Badajoz (white and black).

GALICIA

COMMUNITY FLAG

Adopted 5 May 1984. Proportions 2:3.

White and blue are the colours of the Virgin Mary. The design of the flag is based on that of the maritime flag of the city of La Coruña.

LA RIOJA

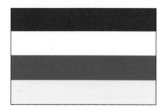

COMMUNITY FLAG

Adopted 31 May 1985. Proportions 2:3.

The colours are taken from the first field of the regional arms. (Above a green mountain on a golden (yellow) field is a red cross between two silver (white) shells.)

MADRID

COMMUNITY FLAG

Adopted 25 February 1983. Proportions 7:11.

Red is the colour of Castile. The stars appear in the arms of the city of Madrid.

MURCIA

COMMUNITY FLAG

Adopted 9 June 1982. Proportions 2:3.

The castles recall that Murcia once belonged to Castile. The seven crowns stand for the seven provinces of Murcia.

NAVARRE

COMMUNITY FLAG

Adopted 10 August 1982. Proportions 2:3.

The flag displays the shield of the arms of Navarre, which date from the 13th century, ensigned with the royal crown.

VALENCIA

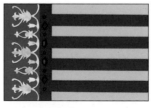

COMMUNITY FLAG

Adopted 1 July 1982. Proportions 2:3.

The flag is almost an exact copy of the flag granted by King James I the Conqueror to the City of Valencia in 1238.

ANDORRA

Principality of Andorra, Catalonian **Principat d'Andorra**, Spanish **Principado de Andorra**, French **Principauté d'Andorre**.
Independent co-principality in the Pyrenees, SW Europe.

NATIONAL FLAG

Adopted in present form in 1993. Proportions 2:3.

The blue-yellow-red tricolour has been in use since the second half of the 19th century. Blue and red are the colours of France, yellow and red are those of Spain, and together they reflect Franco-Spanish protection. The arms combine the arms of the bishopric of Urgel, the counts of Foix, Catalonia and Béarn. The motto is "United strength is stronger".

MONACO

Principality of Monaco,
French **Principauté de Monaco**.
Constitutional monarchy under French protectorate, SW Europe.

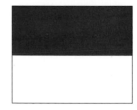

CIVIL FLAG AND ENSIGN

Adopted 4 April 1881. Proportions 4:5.

The colours are those of the ducal arms of Grimaldi (lozengy (diamond-shaped) white and red). Since the 17th century the flag has been white with the shield of arms.

SOUTH AND SOUTH-EAST EUROPE

ITALY

Republic of Italy, Italian **Repubblica Italiana**.
Republic in S Europe.

CIVIL ENSIGN

Officially adopted 19 June 1946. Proportions 2:3.
The state and civil flag is without arms.

Originally this was the national flag of the
Cisalpine Republic, founded by Napoleon.
The flag's design was influenced by the
French *Tricolore* and was in use from
11 May 1798 to 20 August 1802. It was
reintroduced in 1848 by the King of
Sardinia, who charged the white stripe with
his arms of Savoy and in 1861 this became
the national flag of the united Italy. In
1946 the arms were removed from the flag.

VATICAN

Holy See, Vatican City State, Italian **Santa
Sede, Stato della Cittá del Vaticano**.
Papal state in S Europe.

STATE FLAG

Officially adopted 7 June 1929. Proportions 1:1.

A flag of this design was introduced as the
merchant flag of the Pontifical State at the
beginning of the 19th century. The colours
are those of the keys of St Peter, which are
the keys to the kingdom of heaven and a
symbol of papal authority. The crossed keys

with the papal tiara have been the emblem
of the papal state since the 14th century.
Although the official proportions are
1:1, the actual flags flown in the Vatican
City are 2:3.

SAN MARINO

Most Serene Republic of San Marino, Italian
Serenissima Repubblica di San Marino.
Republic in central Italian peninsula, S Europe.

STATE FLAG

Adopted 6 April 1862. Proportions 3:4.
Civil flag is without arms.

As an emblem of sovereignty, San Marino
adopted in 1797 a white and blue national
cockade. The colours were taken from the
coat of arms, which displays three white
towers on a blue field. The towers represent
three castles built on three summits of
Mount Titano: Guaita, Cesta and Montale.
The white stands for peace, exemplified by
the white clouds and the snow; the blue is a
symbol of liberty and the sky over San Marino.

MALTA

Republic of Malta,
Maltese **Repubblika Ta'Malta**.
Insular republic in the Mediterranean, S Europe.

NATIONAL FLAG

Adopted 21 September 1964. Proportions 2:3.

The colours are those of the Knights of St
John of Jerusalem (the white Maltese cross
on a red field), who ruled Malta from 1530
to 1798. In April 1942 King George VI of
the United Kingdom awarded the islanders
the George cross for heroism in World War
II. Since 1964 the George cross bordered in
red has been placed directly on the
white field.

SLOVENIA

Republic of Slovenia, Slovene **Republika
Slovenija**. Republic in S Europe.

NATIONAL FLAG AND ENSIGN

Adopted 24 June 1991. Proportions 1:2.

The national flag, showing the same
arrangement of the pan-Slavic colours as
the flags of Russia or Slovakia, was adopted
by the Slovenian patriots in 1848. In 1991
the newly created arms of Slovenia were
added to the tricolour of white-blue-red.
The main feature of the arms is a stylized
silhouette of Triglav, the highest mountain
in the Slovene Alps. The three yellow stars
on a blue field are from the arms of the
former Duchy of Celje. The wavy lines
symbolize the rivers and the Adriatic Sea.

CROATIA

Republic of Croatia, Croat **Republika
Hrvatska**. Republic in S Europe.

NATIONAL FLAG

Adopted 22 December 1990. Proportions 1:2.

Following the example of other Slavic nations, the Croats in 1848 adopted a red-white-blue horizontal tricolour. When Croatia proclaimed independence in 1941, the arms (checked white and red) were placed in the centre of the tricolour and the badge of Ustasha in the canton. Under communist rule the Croat tricolour was charged with a red star.

The crown surmounting the present state arms is composed of shields with the historic arms of Croatia (golden star above silver crescent), Dubrovnik (two red stripes on a blue field), Dalmatia (three golden lions' heads), Istria (golden goat with red horns and hooves) and Slavonica (golden star above red stripe, fimbriated silver, and charged with black marten).

BOSNIA-HERZEGOVINA

Republic of Bosnia-Herzegovina,
Serbian and Croat **Bosna i Hercegovina**.
Federal republic in S Europe.

NATIONAL FLAG AND ENSIGN

Adopted 4 February 1998. Proportions 1:2.

This flag was one of three proposals presented to parliament by a commission appointed by a special envoy of the United Nations. All three employed the same colours; the blue was to stand for the United Nations but it was changed to a darker blue to correspond with the European Union flag. The blue and the stars represent Europe and the yellow, the colour of the sun, symbolizes hope. The triangle stands for the three ethnic groups: Muslims, Croats and Serbs.

TERRITORIES OF BOSNIA AND HERZEGOVINA

After the civil war, on the basis of the 1996 agreement reached in Dayton (Ohio), Bosnia and Herzegovina was transformed into a federal state with two autonomous provinces.

CROAT-MUSLIM FEDERATION

NATIONAL FLAG

Adopted 6 November 1996. Proportions 2:3.

Red stands for the Croats, green for the Bosnian people and white for purity and peace. The golden fleur-de-lis is from the arms of Tvrtko, who was crowned in 1376 as Stephen I, King of Bosnia, Serbia and the sea-coast. It is a symbol of the Bosnians, while the historic arms of Croatia represent the Croat population. The ten stars symbolize the ten provinces that make up the Federation.

SERBIAN REPUBLIC

NATIONAL FLAG

Adopted 9 January 1992. Proportions 1:2.

The tricolour has the Serbian historic arms in the centre, a golden cross with four golden flints each resembling the Cyrillic letter "S". They stand for the first letters of the Serbian motto, which translates as: "Only unity will save the Serbs".

YUGOSLAVIA

Federal Republic of Yugoslavia, Serbian **Federativna Republika Jugoslavija**.
Federal republic in SE Europe.

NATIONAL FLAG AND CIVIL ENSIGN

Adopted 1 December 1918, readopted 27 April 1992. Proportions 1:2.

From 1918 to 1941 the Yugoslav version of the pan-Slavic tricolour without any emblem was the civil flag and ensign. Under communist rule the national flag and civil ensign used the same tricolour, which from 1945 to 1946 was charged with a red star and from 1946 to 1992 with the red star bordered in yellow.

YUGOSLAVIAN REPUBLICS

From 1945 to 1991 Yugoslavia comprised six republics; now only two remain: Serbia and Montenegro.

SERBIA

STATE AND NATIONAL FLAGS

Introduced 28 January 1839, re-adopted 1992. Proportions 1:2.

The first Serbian horizontal tricolour of pan-Slavic colours, introduced in 1835, was white-blue-red. In 1838 the present order of colours was adopted, and in this form the tricolour served as the national flag of semi-independent Serbia and of the kingdom of Serbia (1882–1918).

MONTENEGRO

NATIONAL FLAG

Introduced in 1992. Proportions 1:3.

The flag is identical to that of Serbia, but it has different proportions. From 1860 to 1918 the same tricolour, but with the proportions 2:3, was the civil flag of the kingdom of Montenegro.

ALBANIA

Republic of Albania,
Albanian **Republika e Shqipërisë**.
Republic in SE Europe.

NATIONAL FLAG

*Adopted 28 February 1912, re-established
7 April 1992. Proportions 5:7.*

The red banner with the black double-headed eagle was the ensign of George Castriota, known as Skanderbeg, the hero of the uprising against the Turks and founder of the independent state in 1443. He probably chose the eagle on account of a tradition that the Albanians are the descendants of the eagle. They call themselves *Shkypetars* which translates as: "the sons of the eagle".

MACEDONIA

Republic of Macedonia, Macedonian
Republika Makedonija.
Republic in SE Europe.

NATIONAL FLAG

Adopted 5 October 1995. Proportions 1:2.

This is the second national flag of Macedonia since the country proclaimed independence in 1991. The first flag was surrounded by controversy and was abandoned after 3 years. The present flag displays a yellow sun of eight rays instead of the former Star of Vergina with 16 rays.

GREECE

Hellenic Republic,
Greek **Elliniki Dimokratia**.
Republic in SE Europe.

NATIONAL FLAG AND ENSIGN

*Adopted 15 March 1822, re-introduced
21 December 1978. Proportions 2:3.*

The common device of all the flags used in the war for independence in 1821 was a white cross, the symbol of Christian faith. When in 1822 the Greek government adopted flags for the Army, and merchant and war ensigns, all of them displayed the same Greek cross. The flag of the Navy, and the later flag used on land, was a blue square with a white cross. The war ensign, in use until 1833, was the same design as the present national flag.

The nine stripes represent the nine syllables of the war cry of independence, *Eleutheria i Thanatos* ("Freedom or Death"). The blue stands for the pure Greek sky, and recalls that God inspired the Greek people to fight for independence in spite of all odds. The white symbolizes the purity and sacred character of the struggle for liberation from Turkish tyranny.

MOUNT ATHOS

Greek **Hagion Oros**.
Self-governing theocratic republic under Greek protectorate, SE Europe.

STATE FLAG

*Date of introduction unknown.
Proportions 2:3.*

The first monastery on Mount Athos, the Great Laura, was founded in AD 963 by St Athanasius the Athonite. In the 11th century several more monasteries were built with the help of the Byzantine Empire, and in 1060 the Byzantine Emperor gave the monastic community its first constitution.

The golden yellow flag is charged with the black Byzantine eagle holding an orb and a sword in its claws. An imperial crown appears above its two heads.

BULGARIA

Republic of Bulgaria,
Bulgarian **Republika Bulgariya**.
Republic in SE Europe.

NATIONAL FLAG AND CIVIL ENSIGN

Adopted in 1878, re-introduced 22 November 1990. Proportions 3:5.

Because Russia supported the Bulgarians in their struggle for independence from Turkey, the Constitutional Assembly adopted an almost identical tricolour, although this one had a green stripe in place of the blue one. The colour of the new green stripe symbolizes freedom. The white symbolizes peace and Slavic thought, and the red represents the bravery of the Bulgarian people. Under communist rule (from 1947–1990) the state emblem was displayed on the white stripe near the hoist.

ROMANIA

Romania, Romanian **România**.
Republic in SE Europe.

NATIONAL FLAG, CIVIL AND STATE ENSIGN

Introduced in 1848, adopted in 1867, re-adopted 27 December 1989. Proportions 2:3.

Blue, yellow and red are the colours of the arms of the principalities of Walachia (red and yellow) and Moldavia (red and blue). These colours appeared together for the first time in 1848 on a revolutionary vertical tricolour of blue-yellow-red which was based on the French *Tricolore*. Walachia and Moldavia united in 1861 under the name of Romania, and adopted a red-yellow-blue horizontal tricolour. In April 1867 the colours were reversed and arranged vertically. From 1867 to 1989 the state flag was always charged with the actual state arms.

NORTHERN CYPRUS

Turkish Republic of Northern Cyprus,
Turkish **Kibris Cumhuriyeti**.
Republic in NE part of the island of Cyprus, SE Europe and W Asia.

NATIONAL FLAG

*Adopted 13 March 1984.
Proportions 2:3.*

The national flag of Northern Cyprus retains the white field of the flag of Cyprus. The crescent with the star is the symbol of Islam.

CYPRUS

Greek Republic of Cyprus,
Greek **Kypriaki Dimokratia**.
Republic in NW and S part of the island of Cyprus, SE Europe and W Asia.

NATIONAL FLAG AND ENSIGN

Adopted 16 August 1960. Proportions 3:5..

The map of the island is dark yellow, symbolizing copper which has been mined here since the 3rd millennium BC. Copper takes its name from the Greek name for the island, *Kupros*, and the crossed olive branches stand for peace between the Greeks and Turks. The white is also a symbol of peace.

TURKEY

Republic of Turkey,
Turkish **Türkiye Cumhuriyeti**.
Republic in SE Europe and W Asia.

NATIONAL FLAG AND ENSIGN

Adopted in 1793, officially confirmed 5 June 1936. Proportions 2:3.

Red was the colour of Umar I, the caliph who ruled from AD 634 to 644 and was known as a great consolidator of the Islamic Empire. In the 14th century red became the colour of the Ottoman Empire. The crescent and star is the symbol of Islam.

MOLDOVA

Republic of Moldova,
Moldovan **Republica Moldoveneasca**.
Republic in E Central Europe.

NATIONAL FLAG

Adopted 12 May 1990. Proportions 2:3.

In 1940 Bessarabia and Bukowina, a substantial part of historic Moldavia, were torn out of Romania and forcibly incorporated into the Soviet Union under the name of the Moldavian SSR. Striving for independence and eventual reunification with Romania, the Moldavian authorities adopted the flag of Romania and charged it with the state arms (the eagle of Walachia with the shield of Moldavia).

MOLDOVAN TERRITORIES

The Gagauzians and the inhabitants of the territory east of the Dniester river were proclaimed independent republics in 1990 and 1992 respectively. Since 1994, Gagauzia has been an autonomous part of Moldova. The status of the Trans-Dniester Republic is not clear.

GAGAUZIA

NATIONAL FLAG

Adopted 31 October 1995. Proportions 1:2.

Blue is the traditional colour of the Turkic peoples. It symbolizes the sky, hope, kind-heartedness and allegiance to the Fatherland. For the Turkic people the white represents the west and symbolizes where the Gagauzians live; it is also a symbol of friendly co-existence with the Moldavians, Bulgarians, Ukrainians and Russians. The red is a symbol of gallantry and courage in the fight for freedom; it stands for the rebirth of the Gagauzians as a nation and represents their generosity. The three stars represent their past, present and future.

TRANS-DNIESTER REPUBLIC

NATIONAL FLAG

Date of introduction unknown. Proportions 1:2.

This former territory of the Moldavian SSR on the east side of the river Dniester and inhabited mainly by Russians and Ukrainians, proclaimed independence on 2 September 1991. It retained the Soviet flag but several years later removed the hammer and sickle.

UKRAINE

Ukrainian **Ukraina**.
Republic in E Central Europe.

NATIONAL FLAG AND CIVIL ENSIGN

Adopted 1918, re-adopted 21 January 1992.
Proportions 2:3.

The national colours derive from the arms of the medieval principality of Galicia (golden lion on a blue field). The first Ukrainian flag, adopted by the Supreme Council in 1848, was a yellow-blue horizontal bicolour and this was the first flag of the independent Ukraine, adopted in January 1918. However, in the 19th century most of the flags displayed by the public were bicolours, with the blue at the top, and this order of colours has been official since March 1918. The blue stands for the sky and the yellow for wheat, the main source of the wealth of Ukraine.

AUTONOMOUS TERRITORY

The only autonomous part of Ukraine is Crimea. The peninsula was conquered and settled by Tartars in the 13th century, annexed by Russia in 1783 and transferred in 1954 from the Russian SFSR to the Ukrainian SSR. It proclaimed independence on 5 May 1992 under the name of the Crimean Republic but later agreed to be an autonomous part of the Ukraine.

CRIMEA

NATIONAL FLAG

Adopted 24 September 1992. Proportions 1:2.

The Crimea was transferred in 1954 from the Russian SFSR to the Ukrainian SSR. It proclaimed independence on 5 May 1992 but later agreed to be an autonomous part of Ukraine. The flag displays the Russian colours in a different order. The colours represent the future (blue), the present (white), and the Crimea's heroic and tragic past (red).

BELARUS

Republic of Belarus,
Belorussian **Respublika Belarus**.
Republic in E Central Europe.

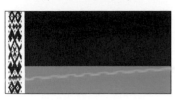

NATIONAL FLAG

Introduced 7 June 1995. Proportions 1:2.

When Belarus proclaimed independence in 1991 it readopted the white-red-white tricolour, first introduced in 1918. This was used in great numbers during rallies and demonstrations against the regime of the pro-Russian president. In response a presidential decree was issued introducing the current flag, which is similar to the flag of Soviet Belorussia (1951–1991). A white and red national ornament appears on the vertical stripe at the hoist.

RUSSIA

Russian Federation,
Rusian **Rossiyskaya Federatsiya**.
Federal republic in E Europe and N Asia.

NATIONAL FLAG AND CIVIL ENSIGN

Introduced 1699, re-adopted 22 August 1991.
Proportions 2:3 (decreed 11 December 1993).

The Russian civil ensign was personally designed by Peter the Great, Tsar of Russia, in 1699 and became the national flag of Russia on 7 May 1883. In 1918 it was replaced by a red flag with the golden initials RSFSR in the upper hoist. Since 1990 the white-blue-red tricolour has been used in great numbers by pro-democracy forces.

RUSSIAN REPUBLICS

According to the constitution Russia comprises 21 republics, 49 provinces, six territories, ten administrative areas, two cities with federal status and one autonomous region. Flags of 20 republics follow. Since Chechnya is a de facto independent former republic and did not sign the Russian constitution, it is shown separately.

ADYGEA

NATIONAL FLAG

Adopted in 1830, re-adopted 24 March 1992.
Proportions 1:2.

The green is a symbol of Islam; the 12 stars recall the tribes of Adygeans, united in the 19th century in the struggle for independence. The arrows originally symbolized the brotherhood and bravery of those tribes; today they symbolize the brotherhood and unity of all nationalities in Adygea.

ALANIA

NATIONAL FLAG

Adopted 10 December 1991. Proportions 1:2.

The white and red reflect qualities of the Alanian people – ethical purity and gallantry respectively. The yellow stands for abundance and prosperity.

ALTAY

NATIONAL FLAG

Adopted 2 July 1992. Proportions 1:2.

The white symbolizes faithfulness, as well as mutual understanding between the various nationalities of Altay. The blue stands for the purity of the skies, mountains, rivers and lakes.

BASHKORTOSTAN

NATIONAL FLAG

Adopted 25 February 1992. Proportions 1:2.

The stylized *kurai* flower (*Salsola kali*) is a symbol of friendship. Its seven petals represent the tribes who laid foundations of unity and consolidation for the Bashkir people. The blue symbolizes the integrity and virtue of the thoughts of the people; the white represents their peacefulness, openness and readiness to co-operate; the green stands for freedom and eternal life.

BURYATIA

NATIONAL FLAG

Adopted 29 October 1992. Proportions 1:2.

The traditional Buryat *Soyonbo*, consisting of the moon, sun and fire, is a symbol of eternal life. The blue stands for the sky and Lake Baykal, the white symbolizes purity, and the yellow represents freedom and prosperity.

CHUVASHIA

NATIONAL FLAG

Adopted 29 April 1992. Proportions 5:8.

The main charge of the flag is a stylized tree of life, a symbol of rebirth, with the three suns, a traditional emblem popular in Chuvash art. The purple stands for the land, the golden yellow for prosperity.

DAGESTAN

NATIONAL FLAG

Adopted 26 February 1994. Proportions 1:2.

The green is the symbol of Islam, the blue represents the Caspian Sea and the red stands for courage and fidelity.

INGUSHETIA

NATIONAL FLAG

Adopted 15 July 1994. Proportions 1:2.

In the religion and philosophy of the Ingushetians, the solar emblem (in the centre of the flag) represents not only the sun and the universe but also awareness of the oneness of the spirit in the past, present and future.

The red recalls the struggle of the Ingush people for existence and in the defence of their homeland. The white symbolizes the divine purity of the thoughts and views of the nation. The green is the symbol of Islam.

KABARDINO-BALKARIA

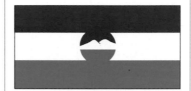

NATIONAL FLAG

Adopted 21 July 1994. Proportions 1:2.

The blue stands for the sky, the white represents the snow-topped Caucasus Mountains and the green symbolizes the fields. In the centre is a white silhouette of Mount Elbrus, the highest peak in Europe.

KALMYKIA

NATIONAL FLAG

Adopted 30 July 1993. Proportions 1:2.

The yellow stands for the sun, the people and the religious faith of the nation. The blue represents the sky, eternity and steadiness. The lotus is a symbol of purity, spiritual rebirth and happiness. Its five upper petals represent the continents and the lower four stand for the quarters of the globe. Together they symbolize the will of the Kalmyks to live in friendship and to co-operate with all the nations of the world.

KARACHAYEVO-CHERKESIYA

NATIONAL FLAG

Adopted 3 February 1994. Proportions 1:2.

The blue is the colour of peace, good intentions and serenity. The green represents nature, fertility and wealth; it is the colour of youth, and also of wisdom and restraint. The red is a symbol of warmth and friendship between nations. The sun rising above the mountains represents the hope of the peoples in the Caucasus for a bright future.

KARELIA

NATIONAL FLAG

Adopted 16 February 1993. Proportions 2:3.

Warm feelings, unity and co-operation between the peoples of Karelia are represented by the red stripe. The blue stands for the lakes and the green for the forests.

KHAKASSIA

NATIONAL FLAG

Adopted 8 July 1992. Proportions 1:2.

The use of the Russian colours shows that the republic is part of the Russian Federation. The green, the traditional colour of Siberia, is a symbol of eternal life and rebirth. The emblem is a sign of respect to the ancestors who used the solar symbol; its black colour symbolizes their wisdom.

KOMI

NATIONAL FLAG

Adopted 27 November 1991. Proportions 1:2.

The colours of the flag reflect the geographical location of the republic and its physical features. The blue stands for the sky, the green for the taiga landscape and the white for the snow.

MARI EL

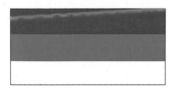

NATIONAL FLAG

Adopted 3 September 1992. Proportions 1:2.

The colours are those of Russia but in different shades. The name of the republic appears below a solar sign, which is part of the traditional national emblem.

MORDOVIA

NATIONAL FLAG

Adopted 30 March 1995. Proportions 1:2.

This republic uses the national colours of Russia in different shades. A local form of the solar emblem is placed in the centre.

SAKHA

NATIONAL FLAG

Adopted 14 December 1992. Proportions 1:2.

The white disc represents the northern sun. The blue, white and green stand for the sky, snow and taiga landscape. The red symbolizes the courage and constancy of the people.

TATARSTAN

NATIONAL FLAG

Adopted 29 November 1991. Proportions 1:2.

The green, the colour of Islam, represents the Tatars; the red stands for the Russians. The white stripe symbolizes peace between the Tatar majority and the Russian minority.

TUVA

NATIONAL FLAG

Adopted 17 September 1992. Proportions 1:2.

Three days after it was adopted this flag was consecrated by the Dalai Lama, who was visiting Tuva at the time. The colours stand for prosperity (yellow), courage and strength (blue), and purity (white).

UDMURTIA

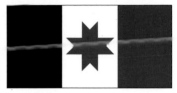

NATIONAL FLAG

Adopted 3 December 1993. Proportions 1:2.

The black is a symbol of the earth and of stability, the white stands for the universe and the purity of moral foundations, and the red represents the sun and life. The solar emblem protects the people against ill fortune.

CHECHNYA

Chechen Republic,
Chechen **Republika Ichkeriya**.
De facto independent former republic of Russia in the Caucasus Mountains, E Europe.

NATIONAL FLAG

Adopted 2 November 1991. Proportions 2:3.

The green is the colour of Islam, the red symbolizes the blood shed in the struggle for independence and the white represents the road to a bright future.

Flags of Asia

Illustrated here are the current national flags of the countries of Asia, from Georgia and Abkhazia to South Korea and Japan, as well as the flags of their territories, states and provinces.

Because Asia is so vast, we have grouped together its countries into geographical sections. We begin in western Asia, then move on to the Middle East, South-west Asia and then Central Asia. Finally, we look at the flags of the countries of southern and South-east Asia and the Far East. There are some geographical anomalies: the flags of Russia, Turkey, Cyprus and Northern Cyprus can all be found in *Flags of Europe*.

For each entry, the country or territory's name is given in its most easily recognized form and then in all its official languages. This is followed by a description of its political status and geographic position. The basic data for each flag contains the status of the flag, date of adoption, proportions, and the symbolic meaning.

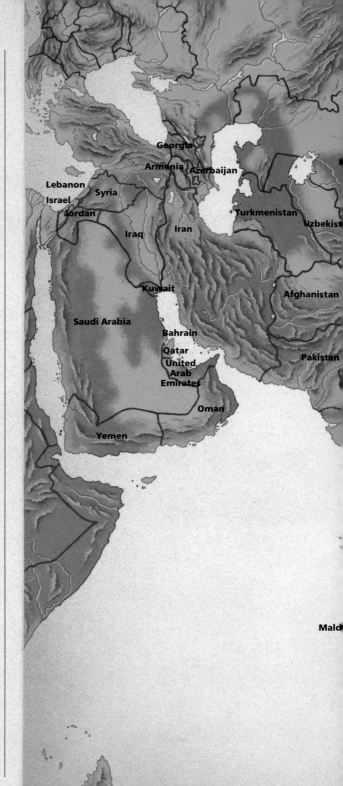

WESTERN ASIA

GEORGIA

Republic of Georgia,
Georgian **Sakartvelos Respublika**.
Republic in W Asia.

NATIONAL FLAG AND CIVIL ENSIGN

*Introduced 25 March 1918, re-adopted
14 November 1990. Proportions 3:5.*

Dogwood red is the national colour of
Georgia. The black and white represent the
tragic past under Russian rule and hope for
a peaceful future.

ABKHAZIA

Republic of Abkhazia,
Abkhaz **Arespublika Apsňi**.
De facto independent former autonomous
republic in Georgia, W Asia.

NATIONAL FLAG

Adopted 23 July 1992. Proportions 2:3.

The design of the flag is based on the flag
of North Caucasia, which was in use
1918–1919. The palm of a hand was a
symbol of Abkhaz statehood in the
8th–10th centuries and the stars and stripes
represent the seven historic districts of
Abkhazia. (Seven is a sacred number, often
found in Abkhaz mythology, religion and
folk art.) The stripes in green and white
symbolize the tolerance of the Caucasus

people and the peaceful co-existence of
Islam (green) and Christianity (white).

ARMENIA

Republic of Armenia,
Armenian **Haikakan Hanrapetoutioun**.
Republic in W Asia.

NATIONAL FLAG AND ENSIGN

*Introduced 22 April 1918, re-adopted
1 September 1991. Proportions 1:2.*

The red recalls the blood shed in the
struggle for national existence. The blue
stands for the skies, hope and the
unchanging character of the land. The
orange represents the courage of the people.

NAGORNO-KARABAKH

Armenian **Artsakh**
De facto independent former autonomous
republic of Azerbaijan, W Asia.

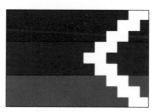

NATIONAL FLAG

Adopted in June 1992. Proportions unspecified.

The flag displays the colours of Armenia but
has slightly different symbolic meaning: the
blood spilt in the struggle to preserve the
nation (red), love of liberty (blue) and bread
(orange). The westwards-pointing arrow is
a graphic representation of the country's
current separation from Armenia proper and
its hopes for union with the Fatherland.

AZERBAIJAN

Republic of Azerbaijan,
Azeri **Azarbajchan Respublikasy**.
Republic in W Asia.

NATIONAL FLAG AND ENSIGN

Adopted 5 February 1991. Proportions 1:2.

The main features of the flag are based on
the flag introduced in autumn 1917 and
used until the occupation of the country
by the Red Army in 1920. The colours
represents the Turkic world (blue),
contemporary life (red) and the Islamic
religion (green). The crescent and star is
the symbol of Islam. The eight points
of the star stand for the Turkic peoples:
Azerbaijani, Ottoman, Jagatay, Tatar,
Kazakh, Kipchak, Seljuk and Turkoman.

THE REGION OF CAUCASIA

The republics on this page belong to
the region of Caucasia which comprises
13 political entities including Chechnya,
six Russian republics (Adygea, Alania,
Dagestan, Ingushetia, Kabardino-
Balkaria, Karachayevo-Cherkesiya) and
South Ossetia, an autonomous
subdivision of Georgia. It is home to
over 40 different nations and ethnic
groups of which only a few had or have
their own states.

The flag of the Balkars is in the
section *Flags of Peoples and Causes:
Nations and ethnic groups*. There are
also historic flags, not depicted here,
for the flags of the Soviet Republics of
Armenia, Azerbaijan Georgia and
others. These are prevalently red but in
other respects bear little resemblance to
those of today.

SYRIA

Republic of Syria,
Arabic **al-Jumhuriya al-Arabiya as-Suriya**.
Republic in W Asia.

NATIONAL FLAG AND ENSIGN

Adopted 30 March 1980. Proportions 2:3.

The present flag is that of the United Arab Republic, used from 1958 to 1961 in both Syria and Egypt. In 1972 Egypt, Syria and Libya formed the Federation of Arab Republics, with a common flag. The policy of reconciliation between Egypt and Israel caused Libya to withdraw from the Federation in 1977, and Syria followed suit in 1980. The Syrian authorities changed the flag because they felt that the Federation flag had been disgraced when it was dipped to the Prime Minister of Israel by an Egyptian guard of honour.

LEBANON

Republic of Lebanon,
Arabic **al-Jumhuriya al-Lubnaniya**.
Republic in W Asia.

NATIONAL FLAG AND ENSIGN

Adopted 7 December 1943. Proportions 2:3.

The red symbolizes sacrifices in the struggle for independence, and the white stands for purity and peace. The cedar is a symbol of holiness, eternity and peace, and since the 19th century it has been the symbol of the Maronite Christian community in Lebanon.

ISRAEL

State of Israel, Hebrew **Medinat Israel**.
Republic in W Asia.

NATIONAL FLAG

Adopted 28 October 1948. Proportions 8:11.

The flag was designed for the Zionist movement in 1891. The basic design recalls the *tallith*, the Jewish prayer shawl, which is white with blue stripes. The hexagram in the centre is the *Magen David* ("Shield of David"), often erroneously called the Star of David. It became the Jewish symbol in the 17th century and was adopted by the First Zionist Congress in 1897.

PALESTINE

State of Palestine,
Arabic **Daulat Filastin**.
Semi-autonomous state comprising Gaza and part of the West Bank of Jordan in W Asia.

NATIONAL FLAG

Introduced 1922. Proportions 1:2.

The flag is based on a flag used in the Arab revolt of 1917 and displays the pan-Arab colours.

JORDAN

Hashemite Kingdom of Jordan, Arabic **al-Mamlaka al-Urdunniya al-Hashemiya**.
Constitutional monarchy in W Asia.

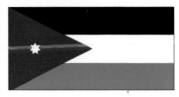

NATIONAL FLAG, CIVIL AND STATE ENSIGN

Introduced in 1921, officially confirmed 16 April 1928. Proportions 1:2.

The flag displays the pan-Arab colours, with the seven points of the star representing the seven verses that make up the *Fatiha* of the Koran: the Fundamental Law of Life, Thought and Aspiration.

SAUDI ARABIA

Kingdom of Saudi Arabia,
Arabic **al-Mamlaka al-Arabiya as-Saudiya**.
Absolute monarchy in SW Asia.

NATIONAL FLAG

Introduced in 1932, present design adopted 15 March 1973. Proportions 2:3.

The flag is very similar to that of the Wahabi sect, in use since 1901. The green is the colour of Islam. The inscription in white *tulth* script reads "There is no God but Allah and Muhammad is the Prophet of Allah", the Muslim Statement of Faith. The sword is a symbol of justice.

YEMEN

Republic of Yemen,
Arabic **al-Jumhuriya al-Yamaniya.**
Republic in SW Asia.

NATIONAL FLAG AND CIVIL ENSIGN

Adopted 22 May 1990. Proportions 2:3.

After the unification of North and South Yemen, the flag retained the common element of stripes in the pan-Arab colours.

OMAN

Sultanate of Oman, Arabic **Saltanat Uman.**
Absolute monarchy in SW Asia.

NATIONAL FLAG AND ENSIGN

Adopted 18 November 1995. Proportions 1:2.

The national emblem of Oman is composed of two crossed swords surmounted by a ceremonial dagger and an ornate belt. The white symbolizes peace and prosperity. The red is the colour of the pre-1970 Omani flag, which was plain red, and recalls the battles against the foreign invaders. The green represents the Jebel Akhdar (the Green Mountains) and stands for fertility.

UNITED ARAB EMIRATES

Arabic **Dawlat Ittihad al-Imarat al-Arabiyah al-Muttahidah.**
Federal monarchy in SW Asia.

NATIONAL FLAG AND CIVIL ENSIGN

Adopted 2 December 1971, officially hoisted 1 January 1972. Proportions 1:2.

The flag displays the pan-Arab colours. Red is the traditional colour of the emirates and red flags of several tiny Arab states along the southern coast of the Persian Gulf were modified for the first time in 1820 following the General Treaty that was signed by the British and the rulers of eight sheikhdoms. It required that these states "should carry by land and sea a red flag, with or without letters on it, at their option, and this shall be in a border of white". Such were the flags of Sharjah and Ras al Khaimah, while Abu Dhabi, Ajman, Dubai and Umm al Qaiwain used a red flag with a white vertical stripe along the hoist. In 1958 Abu Dhabi exchanged the white stripe for a white canton and in 1961 the flag of Umm al Qaiwain was charged with a white crescent and star. In 1975 the ruler of Sharjah decided to replace his emirate's flag with that of the Union.

ABU DHABI

STATE FLAG

AJMAN, DUBAI

STATE FLAG

AL FUJAIRAH

STATE FLAG

RAS AL KHAIMAH

STATE FLAG

UMM AL QAIWAIN

STATE FLAG

QATAR

State of Qatar, Arabic **Dawlat Qatar**.
Absolute monarchy in SW Asia.

NATIONAL FLAG AND ENSIGN

Adopted in 1948. Proportions 11:28.

The flag used in the 19th century was red with a white vertical stripe along the hoist. In the first half of the 20th century the line separating the two colours became serrated, and the name of the country was often inscribed in white on the red portion of the flag. The local red dyes used in making flags darken when exposed to sun, so the red was officially changed to maroon in 1948.

BAHRAIN

State of Bahrain, Arabic **Dawlat al-Bahrayn**.
Absolute emirate in SW Asia.

NATIONAL FLAG AND ENSIGN

*Adopted in 1933, officially confirmed
19 August 1972. Proportions 3:5.*

In the 19th century the flag of Bahrain was red with a white vertical stripe along the hoist. In 1933 the line dividing the colours was serrated to distinguish the flag of Bahrain from those of other Trucial States.

KUWAIT

State of Kuwait, Arabic **Dawlat al-Kuwait**.
Absolute monarchy in SW Asia.

NATIONAL FLAG AND CIVIL ENSIGN

Adopted 7 September 1961. Proportions 1:2.

The flag displays the pan-Arab colours. The black stands for the defeat of the enemy on the battlefield, the red is the blood of the enemy left on the Arab swords. The green represents the fertile land, and the white the pure Arab deeds.

IRAQ

Republic of Iraq,
Arabic **al-Jumhuriya al-Iraqiya**.
Socialist republic in SW Asia.

NATIONAL FLAG AND ENSIGN

Adopted 14 January 1991. Proportions 2:3.

Since 1963 the flag of Iraq has been a red-white-black horizontal tricolour, with three green stars on the white stripe. During the Gulf War, the Revolutionary Command Council chaired by President Saddam Hussein decided to place the words *Allahu Akbar* ("God is Great") between the stars.

IRAN

Islamic Republic of Iran,
Farsi **Jomhori-e-Islami-e-Irân**.
Authoritarian Islamic republic in SW Asia.

NATIONAL FLAG AND ENSIGN

Adopted 29 July 1980. Proportions 4:7.

One of the consequences of the Islamic revolution in Iran was the addition of religious symbols to the Iranian horizontal tricolour. The central emblem is a composite of Arab letters in the form of four crescents and a vertical line in the middle. The five principal parts of the emblem represent the five principles of Islam and together they form the word *Allah*. Other combinations of these elements represent the Book (Koran), the Sword (the symbol of power and solidarity), man's growth, the negation of all idolatrous values, the negation of all powers and super-powers, and the struggle to establish a unified society. The symmetrical form of the emblem signifies balance and equilibrium.

The words *Allahu Akbar* ("God is Great"), written in highly stylized Kufic script, appear 22 times to commemorate Bahman 22, 1357 (11 February 1979), the day of victory for the revolution.

CENTRAL ASIA

TURKMENISTAN

Republic of Turkmenistan,
Turkmen **Türkmenistan.**
Republic in W Central Asia.

NATIONAL FLAG

Adopted 19 February 1992, modified
1 February 1997. Proportions 1:2.

The flag of Turkmenistan has the most intricate design of all national flags in the world. It is also one of the most interesting. The green field with the crescent and stars is clearly the symbol of Islam; the crescent and stars represent faith in a bright future, while the white symbolizes serenity and kind-heartedness. The five stars symbolize the five *velayats* (regions): Ahal, Balkan, Dashhowuy, Lebap and Mary. They also stand for the five senses. The five points of each star symbolize the five states of matter: solid, liquid, gaseous, crystalline and plasmatic.

The vertical stripe along the hoist bears five major *guls* of the Turkmenian carpets. Each *gul* is a symmetrical medallion, in some cases divided into four quarters in counterchanging colours. Major *guls* are repeated in rows or in a chequered pattern on the central field of the carpet, and minor *guls* appear on the border. They reflect the national identity of Turkmenistan where carpets were part of traditional nomadic life, used for floor-covering, furniture, sacks and bags, and to decorate camel and horse trappings.

In 1995 the President of Turkmenistan declared a policy of neutrality, which was acknowledged by a unanimous vote of the United Nations General Assembly on 12 December 1995. To immortalize this, crossed olive branches similar to those on the UN flag were placed below the *guls*. The new law stated, "The State Flag of Turkmenistan is a symbol of the unity and independence of the nation and of the neutrality of the state."

UZBEKISTAN

Republic of Uzbekistan,
Uzbek **Uzbekistan Respublikasy.**
Republic in W Central Asia.

NATIONAL FLAG

Adopted 18 November 1991. Proportions 1:2.

Blue is the colour of the Turkic peoples and also of the banner of Tamerlane, who ruled an Uzbek empire in the 14th century. It is a symbol of eternal skies and of the people as one of the fundamental sources of life. The white signifies peace, the traditional Uzbek wish for a safe journey and striving for purity of thoughts and deeds. The green is the colour of nature, fertility and new life, as well as being the colour of Islam. The red stripes stand for the vital force in all living organisms, which links good and pure ideas with the eternal sky and deeds on earth.

The crescent symbolizes the new republic. The stars stand for the twelve months of the solar Uzbek calendar and are named after the 12 constellations, reflecting the astronomical knowledge of Uzbeks in ancient times.

KAZAKHSTAN

Republic of Kazakhstan,
Kazak **Kazak Respublikasy.**
Republic in W Central Asia.

STATE AND CIVIL FLAG AND ENSIGN

Adopted 4 June 1992. Proportions 1:2.

Blue is the common colour of the Turkic peoples. Here it stands for the endless skies over all people as a symbol of well-being, tranquillity, peace and unity. The sun and a golden eagle represent the love of freedom and the lofty thoughts and ideals of the Kazakhs. Along the hoist is a typical national ornament.

KYRGYZSTAN

Republic of Kyrgyzstan,
Kyrgyz **Kyrgyz Respublikasy.**
Republic in W Central Asia.

NATIONAL FLAG

Adopted 3 March 1992. Proportions 3:5.

The word *kyrgyz* originally meant "red" and red has been the national colour from time immemorial. Red was also the colour of the banner of Manas the Noble, who struggled for unity and formed the Kyrgyz nation. The sun is a symbol of light, eternity and infinite nobility, and the 40 rays stand for the 40 Kyrgyz tribes united by Manas. The sun is charged with a representation of the device covering the roof of a typical *yurt*, the tent used by the Kyrgyz nomads. It symbolizes hearth and home, the unity of time and space, the origin of life and solidarity.

TAJIKISTAN

Republic of Tajikistan,
Tajik **Jumhuri Tojikiston.**
Republic in W Central Asia.

NATIONAL FLAG

Adopted 24 November 1992. Proportions 1:2.

The crown represents the Tajik people. The name is derived from *tajvar*, which means "crowned". In traditional Tajik culture the magic word "seven" is a symbol of perfection, the embodiment of happiness and the provider of virtue. According to Tajik legend, heaven is composed of seven beautiful orchards, separated by seven mountains each with a glowing star on top.

The red is a symbol of the sun and victory; the white stands for purity, cotton and the snow on the mountains, and the green represents the spiritual meaning of Islam and the generosity of nature.

AFGHANISTAN

Islamic Emirate of Afghanistan,
Autocratic Islamic state in Central Asia.

NATIONAL FLAG

Adopted 27 October 1997. Proportions 1:2.

The white flag with the *Shahada* (the Muslim Statement of Faith) in green is the 17th Afghanistan national flag since 1900. This flag, introduced by the Taliban regime, is not yet recognized internationally; the United Nations Headquarters in New York and the Afghan embassies still fly the former green-white-black horizontal

tricolour with the golden national emblem. Since it was impossible to obtain the exact data on design and proportions of the flag of the current regime, the internationally recognized flag is reproduced here.

KASHMIR

Kashmiri **Azad Jammu o Kashmir.**
Northern, autonomous part of Kashmir within Pakistan, Central Asia.

NATIONAL FLAG

Adopted in 1947. Proportions unspecified.

The flag displays the Pakistani colours, white and green, with the symbols of the Muslim majority (crescent and star) and the Hindu and Sikh minorities (a saffron square). The four white stripes symbolize the four main rivers of Kashmir.

JAMMU AND KASHMIR

Kashmiri **Jammu o Kashmir.**
Southern part of Kashmir, state of India, Central Asia.

NATIONAL FLAG

Adopted in 1952. Proportions 2:3.

The native plough is a symbol of labour, and the three stripes represent the three provinces of the state.

AFGHANISTAN: FLAGS REFLECT POLITICAL CHANGES

Political change in countries that gained independence in the 20th century are often reflected in the change of the national flag. In Afghanistan, the Taliban regime's current flag is the 17th national flag since 1900.

The first three flags (1900–1928) were black with three different state emblems. In July 1928 a horizontal black-red-green tricolour was introduced, and in September of the same year these colours were re-arranged vertically. The colours symbolized the past (black), the blood shed for independence (red), and the wealth and hope for the future (green). In January 1929, the black flag was revived but was soon replaced by the vertical tricolour with three different emblems (from October 1930 to 1974).

In 1974 the monarchy was forcibly abolished and the republican regime changed the emblem and restored the horizontal arrangement of the national colours (from April to October 1978 the flag had no emblem). When the communists came to power in October 1978 they adoped a red flag with a new emblem. From 1980-1992, two flags used under the Soviet occupation were horizontal tricolours with an emblem, which until 1987 displayed a red star.

After the liberation of Kabul in 1992 the national flag became a horizontal tricolour of green, white and black with the golden inscription "God is Great" (on the top stripe), and the Muslim Statement of Faith (on the second stripe).

SOUTHERN ASIA

PAKISTAN

Islamic Republic of Pakistan,
Urdu **Islami Jamhuriya e Pakistan**.
Republic in S Asia.

NATIONAL FLAG

Adopted 14 August 1947. Proportions 2:3.

The flag of the All-India Moslem League, introduced in 1906, was green with the white crescent and star, the colours symbolizing Islam. A white vertical stripe at the hoist was added to symbolize the non-Muslim minorities after independence. The white and green portions of the flag symbolize peace and prosperity, the crescent progress and the star light and knowledge.

INDIA

Republic of India, Hindi **Bharatiya Ganarajya.**
Federal republic in S Central Asia.

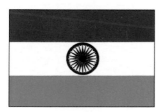

NATIONAL FLAG

Adopted 22 July 1947. Proportions 2:3.

The central figure is *chakra* (wheel) from the capital of the ancient Asokan column at Sarnath. To a Buddhist the wheel represents the inevitability of existence: *Dharma Chakra* (Wheel of Law). The saffron (orange) symbolizes courage and sacrifice, while the white stands for peace and truth, and the green faith and chivalry.

NEPAL

Kingdom of Nepal, Nepali **Nepal Adhirajya**.
Constitutional monarchy in S Central Asia.

NATIONAL FLAG

Adopted 16 December 1962. Proportions 4:3.

Nepal is the only country in the world to have a flag that is not rectangular or square. The two triangles symbolize the Himalaya Mountains and they also stand for two religions, Hinduism and Buddhism. Crimson is the national colour of Nepal. The moon and sun originally symbolized the families of the king and the prime minister, and the wish that the nation might live as long as these celestial bodies.

BHUTAN

Kingdom of Bhutan, Dzongkha **Druk-yul**.
Constitutional monarchy in S Central Asia.

NATIONAL FLAG

In use since the 19th century. Proportions 2:3.

The present design of the flag was established *c*.1965, when the maroon was replaced by orange and the shape of the dragon was modified. The dragon represents the name of the country (*druk* means "dragon") and its colour stands for purity

and loyalty. Its snarling mouth expresses the stern strength of the deities protecting Bhutan, and the jewels clasped in its claws symbolize the wealth and perfection of the country. The yellow stands for the fruitful action of the king in affairs of religion and state; the orange represents religious practice.

BANGLADESH

People's Republic of Bangladesh,
Bengali **Gana Prajatantri Bangladesh**.
Republic in S Asia.

NATIONAL FLAG

Adopted 13 January 1972. Proportions 3:5.

The green represents the greenery of the country, its vitality and youthfulness. The red disc is a symbol of the rising sun of independence after the dark night of a blood-drenched struggle.

SRI LANKA

Democratic Socialist Republic of Sri Lanka,
Sinhala **Sri Lanka prajathanthrika
samajawadi janarajaya**,
Tamil **Ilankayc cananayaka sosalisak
kutiyarucu**.
Socialist republic consisting of an island
in Indian Ocean, S Asia.

NATIONAL FLAG

Adopted 7 September 1978. Proportions 1:2.

In traditional Sanskrit and Pali literature the island is called Sinhaladvipa, the word *sinhala* deriving from the Sinhalese word *sinha* (lion), and since the 15th century a golden lion holding a sword of authority has appeared on the crimson field of the state banner. This flag with a yellow border, a symbol of Buddhism, was adopted as the first flag of independent Ceylon on 4 February 1948. The lion denotes the desire for peace, while the crimson symbolizes national pride. In 1950 the stripes of green (for the Muslims) and saffron (for the Tamils) were added. In 1972 and 1978 the finials in the corners were modified to represent the leaves of the fig tree (*Ficus religiosa*) under which Siddartha Gautama sat when he received enlightenment and became the Buddha. The four leaves stand for love, compassion, sympathy and equanimity, which are virtues extolled by Buddhism.

MALDIVES

Republic of the Maldives,
Divehi **Divehi Rajje ge Jumhuriya**.
Republic comprising 19 clusters of coral islands in Indian Ocean, S Asia.

NATIONAL FLAG AND ENSIGN

Adopted 26 July 1965.
Proportions 2:3.

The crescent is the symbol of Islam. The green stands for peace and prosperity, and the red symbolizes blood shed in the struggle for independence.

BRITISH INDIAN OCEAN TERRITORY

British colony consisting of the Chagos Archipelago in N Indian Ocean.

STATE FLAG AND ENSIGN

Adopted 4 November 1990. Proportions 3:5.
Ensign is in proportions 1:2.

The white and blue wavy stripes represent the Indian Ocean. The palm tree stands for the islands, of which only Diego Garcia is inhabited. The Union flag in the canton and the crown are there to symbolize British sovereignty.

SOUTH-EAST ASIA

MYANMAR

Union of Myanmar, Burmese **Pyidaungsu Myanma Naingngandaw**.
Military republic in SE Asia.

NATIONAL FLAG

Adopted 3 January 1974. Proportions 5:9.

The white represents purity and virtue, the blue symbolizes peace and integrity, and the red signifies courage and decisiveness. The pinion and padi leaves stand for industry and agriculture, and for workers and peasants. The stars represent the 14 constituent member states of the union.

THAILAND

Kingdom of Thailand,
Thai **Muang Thai** or **Pratet Thai**.
Constitutional monarchy in SE Asia.

CIVIL AND STATE FLAG AND ENSIGN

Adopted 28 September 1917. Proportions 2:3.

The flag adopted in 1916 was red with two white stripes, but the central red portion was altered to blue. It was an expression of solidarity with World War I allies (United Kingdom, France, United States and Russia), whose flags used the red, white and blue. The flag is given the name *Trairanga* which means tricolour.

The colours symbolize the blood shed for their country (red), the purity of the people protected by their religion (white) and the monarchy (blue).

CAMBODIA

State of Cambodia,
Khmer **Roat Kampuchea**.
State in Indo-China, SE Asia.

NATIONAL FLAG AND ENSIGN

Adopted 30 June 1993. Proportions 2:3.

The present flag is the seventh since 1948, when the country became independent. All of them except one bore a representation of Angkor Wat, built in the 12th century, which is one of the most impressive temples in the world.

LAOS

Lao People's Democratic Republic, Lao
Sáthálanalat Pasathipatay Pásáson Lao.
Socialist republic in Indo-China, SE Asia.

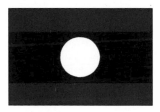

NATIONAL FLAG

Adopted 2 December 1975. Proportions 2:3.

The flag has been used since 1956 by Pathet Lao, the communist guerrilla movement, and became the national flag when it gained control of the country in 1975. The red symbolizes the blood spilt by the Lao people in defence of their Fatherland, the blue stands for the country's wealth, and the white represents the unity of the multi-ethnic society under communist rule.

VIETNAM

Socialist Republic of Vietnam,
Vietnamese **Công Hòa Xã Hội Chu Nghia
Viêt Nam**.
Socialist republic in Indo-China, SE Asia.

NATIONAL FLAG AND ENSIGN

Adopted 30 November 1955. Proportions 2:3.

The red symbolizes the revolution and the blood shed in the struggle for independence. The five-pointed star represents the unity of workers, peasants, intellectuals, young people and soldiers in building socialism.

MACAO

**Macao Special Administrative Region of
the People's Republic of China**.
Former Portuguese colony in SE Asia.

REGIONAL FLAG

*Adopted 31 March 1993, will be in use from
20 December 1999. Proportions 2:3.*

The five stars, taken from the flag of China, recall that Macao is an inseparable part of China. The stylized lotus flower stands for the people, and its three petals represent the three islands of Macao. The bridge and the waves are emblematic of the natural environment surrounding Macao.

HONG KONG

**Hong Kong Special Administrative Region
of the People's Republic of China**.
Former British crown colony in SE Asia.

REGIONAL FLAG

Officially hoisted 1 July 1997. Proportions 2:3.

The stylized bauhinia (orchid tree) flower represents the people of Hong Kong. The five red stars, taken from the flag of China, state that the Territory is an inseparable part of China.

PHILIPPINES

Republic of the Philippines,
Tagalog **Republika ng Pilipinas**.
Republic consisting of an archipelago in the Pacific Ocean, SE Asia.

NATIONAL FLAG AND ENSIGN

*Adopted 19 May 1898. Colours modified
16 September 1997. Proportions 1:2.*

The golden sun with eight rays symbolizes liberty and was championed by the first eight provinces to revolt against Spain. The stars represent the three major regions: Luzon, the Visayas and Mindanao. The white triangle stands for purity and peace while the blue and red symbolize patriotism and bravery respectively. The flag is the only one in the world to change the position of its colours: in time of war the upper stripe is red and the lower blue.

MALAYSIA

Federation of Malaysia,
Malay **Persekutuan Tanah Malaysia**.
Federal constitutional monarchy
in SE Asia.

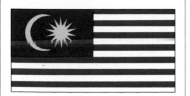

NATIONAL FLAG AND STATE ENSIGN

Adopted 16 September 1963. Proportions 1:2.

The crescent and star is the symbol of
Islam, and the 14 points of the star and the
14 stripes represent the 14 members of the
Federation of Malaysia. (Singapore left the
Federation in 1965 but the flag remains
unchanged.) The blue canton symbolizes the
unity of the peoples of Malaysia and yellow
is the colour of Their Highnesses the rulers.

MALAYSIAN STATES AND TERRITORIES

Malaysia comprises 13 states and two
federal territories (Kuala Lumpur and
Labuan). All flags have the proportions 1:2.
The crescent and star appear on seven flags
and symbolizes Islam, the faith of the
majority of the population.

JOHOR

NATIONAL FLAG AND ENSIGN

Adopted in 1870.

The white and blue represent the ruler and
the government respectively. The red stands
for the warrior caste Hulabalang.

KEDAH

NATIONAL FLAG

Adopted in 1912.

The red is the traditional colour of the
state. The *padi* represents the main crop
of the state, the crescent stands for Islam
and the shield is a symbol of authority.

KELANTAN

NATIONAL FLAG

Adopted in 1924.

The red symbolizes the loyalty of the people
who are faithful to the ruler. The spears and
daggers represent their strength.

KUALA LUMPUR

FLAG OF THE TERRITORY

Adopted on 15 May 1990.

The blue symbolizes the unity of the
population of this federal territory. The
colour red stands for courage and vigour,
the white for purity, and the yellow for
sovereignty and prosperity.

LABUAN

FLAG OF THE TERRITORY

Date of adoption unknown.

The symbolism of the colours is the same as
the national flag.

MELAKA

NATIONAL FLAG

Adopted in 1961.

The colours signify that Melaka is a
component state of Malaysia.

NEGERI SEMBILAN

NATIONAL FLAG

Adopted in 1895.

The colours represent the authorities:
the ruler (yellow), the ruling chiefs of
districts (black), and the people (red).

PAHANG

STATE FLAG

Adopted 28 December 1903.

The white stands for the ruler, whose powers depend on the people. Because white can be changed into any other colour, the ruler can be swayed to meet the wishes of the people. The black represents the people, whose rights should not be alienated by the ruler.

PERAK

STATE FLAG

Adopted c.1920.

The colours represent the authorities – the Sultan (white), the Raja Muda (yellow) and the Raja di-Hilir (black).

PERLIS

STATE FLAG

Adopted in 1870.

The yellow stands for the ruler, the blue represents the people. Together the colours symbolize co-operation between the ruler and his subjects.

PINANG

STATE FLAG

Adopted in 1949.

The tree is *pokok pinang*, the betel nut tree (*Areca catechu*) after which the state is named. The blue represents the sea that surrounds the island, the white stands for the state itself in its serenity and the yellow represents prosperity.

SABAH

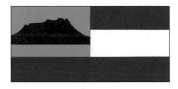

STATE FLAG

Adopted 16 September 1988.

This is the only flag in the world with displays three different shades of blue: royal (silhouette of Mount Kinabalu), icicle (canton) and zircon (upper stripe). Mt Kinabalu represents the state of Sabah. The zircon blue symbolizes peace and tranquillity, the white purity and justice, the red courage and conviction, the icicle blue unity and prosperity, and the royal blue strength and co-operation.

SARAWAK

STATE FLAG

Adopted 31 August 1988.

The flag displays the colours established in 1870 and used until 1973. At that time the flag was yellow charged with a cross divided vertically into black and red portions. The yellow denotes the supremacy of law and order, and unity and stability in diversity. The black represents the natural resources (petroleum, timber etc), that provide the foundation for the advancement of the people. The red stands for the courage, determination and sacrifices of the people in their tireless pursuit to attain and maintain progress and esteem in the course of creating a model state. The star embodies the aspiration of the people to improve their quality of life; its nine points represent the nine divisions of the state.

CHANGING FLAGS

While Johor, Negeri Sembilan and Perlis still use flags adopted more than a hundred years ago, Sabah and Sarawak have changed their flags several times over the last half a century. In the 1980s both states had flags similar to Czechoslovakia's (now the Czech Republic). From 1973 to 1988, the flag of Sarawak had red and white stripes and a blue triangle. From 1982 to 1988, the flag of Sabah had blue and white stripes and a red triangle.

From 1925 to 1933, the national flag of Terengganu was black with a vertical white stripe at the hoist. In 1933 a white Muslim crescent and star was placed in the centre of the black portion of the flag, and in 1947 the design of the flag was changed to the current one.

SELANGOR

STATE FLAG

Adopted in 1965.

The yellow and red symbolize flesh and blood respectively, giving life and strength to the state.

TERENGGANU

STATE FLAG

Adopted in 1947.

The flag is a graphic representation of the protection that the sultan (white) spreads around his subjects (black).

BRUNEI

State of Brunei,
Malay **Negara Brunei Darussalam**.
Absolute monarchy in SE Asia.

STATE FLAG, CIVIL AND STATE ENSIGN

Adopted 29 September 1959. Proportions 1:2.

The flag in its present form, except for the crest, has been in use since 1906 when Brunei became a protected state. The colours are those of the flags of the principal signatories to the agreement between Brunei and the United Kingdom: the Sultan (yellow), Pengiran Bendahara (white) and Pengiran Pemancha (black). The crest was added in 1959. The mast and pedestal represent the three levels of government, and the four feathers symbolize justice, tranquillity, peace and prosperity. The hands signify that the government preserves and promotes the welfare of the citizens. The crescent stands for Islam, the state religion. The state motto, written in Arabic script, means "Always render service by God's guidance". The name of the state appears on the ribbon.

SINGAPORE

Republic of Singapore,
Malay **Repablik Singapura**,
Chinese **Xinjiapo Gongheguo**,
Tamil **Sinkappur Kutijarasu**.
Republic comprising mainly Singapore Island in SE Asia.

STATE FLAG

*Officially hoisted 3 December 1959.
Proportions 2:3.*

The colours represent universal brotherhood (red), and purity and virtue (white). The crescent stands for "a young country on the ascent in its ideals of establishing democratic peace, progress, justice and equality as indicated by the five stars".

INDONESIA

Republic of Indonesia,
Bahasa Indonesia **Republik Indonesia**.
Republic consisting of an archipelago in SE Asia.

NATIONAL FLAG AND ENSIGN

Adopted 17 August 1945. Proportions 2:3.

The flag, officially called *Sang Dwiwarna* (exalted bicolour), symbolizes a living person. The red represents the body and physical life, the white the soul and spiritual life.

STATES OF INDONESIA

Since 1945 Indonesia has been a unitary republic made up of 28 provinces. Before 1945, however, under Dutch rule, Indonesia was composed of more than 200 states, many of which were sultanates. Most of these had their own national flags and ensigns as well as flags of the ruler and other state dignitaries. For example the state of Sambas on the Island of Sumatra had a grand total of 28 distinguishing and rank flags. So, at any time in the 19th century there were thousands of flags in use over vast areas of current Indonesia.

Until 1881, Indonesian seafaring vessels used the flag of whichever state they represented; after this time, however, the Dutch authorities began to enforce the law that they must use the Dutch ensign.

FAR EAST

MONGOLIA

State of Mongolia,
Mongolian **Mongol Uls**.
Republic in E Central Asia.

NATIONAL FLAG

Introduced 12 February 1992. Proportions 1:2.

The basic design of the flag dates from
1940. In 1992 the star surmounting the
emblem was removed and the design of the
Soyonbo, an ancient Mongolian symbol, was
modified. The blue is the traditional colour
of the Mongols and other Turkic peoples
and the two red vertical stripes symbolize the
double joys of liberty and independence.

The *Soyonbo* is accompanied by several
other ancient symbols. The arrowheads, or
triangles, pointing downwards mean "Death
to the enemy"; two signifying "Death to the
enemies of the people". The triangle is a
symbol of straightforwardness, honesty and
adherence to principles. The two fish in
the centre represent men and women. As
fish never sleep they are a reminder that

SOYONBO

Marco Polo was the first European to
report that Mongolian flags were
charged with the sun and moon. In
fact, the ancient sign of *Soyonbo* is
composed of the sun, moon and fire.
Together they represent the wish, "May
you live and flourish forever". Fire
denotes prosperity, regeneration and
ascent, and the three tongues of flame
stand for the past, present and future.
The sun and moon symbolize the belief
that the Mongolians are children of the
sun (mother) and moon (father).

the people should always be vigilant for
their country. The horizontal bars above
and below this image indicate that the
highest and the lowest in society should be
honest and straightforward in the service of
the people. A vertical bar represents a
fortress; the two bars illustrate the proverb,
"Two friends are stronger than stone".

TIBET

Tibetan **Bod rang-skyong ljongs**,
Chinese **Xi-zang**.
Region of China with limited autonomy,
E Central Asia.

CIVIL FLAG

Adopted in 1912. Proportions unspecified.

The white triangle represents a mountain
covered with snow, symbolizing Tibet's
location in the Himalaya Mountains. The
two lions represent harmony between
temporal and spiritual rule. They are
holding the wishing gem. This symbolizes
the rule of law based on the principle of
cause and effect underlying the Ten Golden
Precepts and the Sixteen Humane
Principles of Buddhism, which are the
source of infinite benefit and peace. Above
the gem stand the three flaming jewels",
representing Buddha (God), Dharma (the
Doctrine) and Sangha (the saints, guardians
of the Doctrine).

The sun is a symbol of freedom,
happiness and prosperity. Its 12 rays
represent the 12 descendants of the six
aboriginal tribes of Tibet. Their colours are
symbolic of the two guardian deities (male
and female) protecting the flag. The yellow
border of the flag indicates the spread of the
golden ideals of Buddhism.

CHINA

People's Republic of China,
Chinese **Zhonghua Renmin Gonghe Guo**.
Socialist republic in E and Central Asia.

NATIONAL FLAG AND ENSIGN

Adopted 1 October 1949. Proportions 2:3.

The red stands for the communist
revolution and the large star is a symbol
of the communist party. The four smaller
stars represent the workers, peasants,
bourgeoisie and patriotic capitalists who
are united in building communism.

TAIWAN

Republic of China,
Chinese **Chung Hua Min Kuo**.
Republic consisting of an island in
Pacific Ocean, E Asia.

NATIONAL FLAG AND STATE ENSIGN

Adopted 28 October 1928.
Proportions 2:3.

The flag, adopted as the national flag and
war ensign of China, was retained by the
nationalist forces, which were defeated by
the communists and in 1949 found refuge
on the island of Taiwan. The 12 rays of the
white sun represent the 12 two-hour
periods of the day, and together they
symbolize the spirit of unceasing progress.

The colours stand for the three principles of the people – democracy (blue), the people's livelihood (white) and nationalism (red). The colours also have a dual meaning: blue stands for equality and justice, the white for fraternity and frankness, and the red for liberty and sacrifice.

NORTH KOREA

People's Democratic Republic of Korea, Korean **Chosun Minchu-chui Inmin Konghwa-guk**.
Socialist state in N part of Korean Peninsula, E Asia.

NATIONAL FLAG AND ENSIGN

Adopted 8 September 1948. Proportions 1:2.

The star symbolizes the revolutionary traditions established by President Kim Il Sung. The red represents revolutionary patriotism and the fighting spirit, and the white stands for the Korean nation and its culture. The blue stripes symbolize "the aspiration of the Korean people to unite with the revolutionary people of the whole world and fight for the victory of the idea of independence, friendship and peace".

SOUTH KOREA

Republic of Korea,
Korean **Taehan Min-guk**.
Republic in S part of the Korean Peninsula, E Asia.

NATIONAL FLAG, CIVIL AND STATE ENSIGN

Adopted in 1882, last time modified 21 February 1984. Proportions 2:3.

The white is the Korean national colour, a symbol of purity, peace and justice. The central emblem is a reflection of Chinese cosmogony, in which the opposites of yin and yang unify and co-operate. The yin-yang, a synthesis of the Great Beginning, is called *taeguk* in Korean and from this the flag derives its name *Taeguki*. In the corners are four trigrams, which are also composed of the yin (broken bars) and yang (unbroken bars). Clockwise from the upper hoist, the trigrams symbolize:
(i) heaven, the south and summer,
(ii) the moon, the west, autumn and water,
(iii) the earth, the north and winter, and
(iv) the sun, the east, spring and fire. The black stands for vigilance, perseverance, justice and chastity.

JAPAN

Japanese **Nippon (Nihon)**.
Constitutional monarchy consisting of an island chain in Pacific Ocean, E Asia.

CIVIL AND STATE FLAG AND ENSIGN

Officially adopted 5 August 1854. Proportions 2:3.

This flag, called *Hinomaru* (disc of the sun) has been in use at least since the 14th century. The red sun recalls the name of Japan (the Land of the Rising Sun) and worship of Amaterasu Omikami (the Sun Goddess), the most venerated goddess in the Shinto religion. The colours also reflect the spirit of Shinto ethics, based on a bright, pure, just and gentle heart. The white stands for purity and integrity, the red for sincerity, brightness and warmth.

Flags of Australia and Oceania

The current national flags of the countries of Australasia and Oceania, from Christmas Island and Australia to French Polynesia and the Pitcairn Islands, are illustrated and described in the following pages, together with the flags of their territories, states and provinces.

The countries of this continent, scattered throughout the Pacific Ocean, have been grouped together for ease of reference. We begin in Australia and move swiftly on to the vast Pacific Ocean which is harnessed into the west Pacific, central Pacific, south-west Pacific and finally, the south-east Pacific Ocean.

For each entry, the country or territory's name is given in its most easily recognized form and then in all its official languages. This is followed by a description of its political status and geographic position. The basic data for each flag contains the status of the flag, date of adoption, proportions, and the symbolic meaning.

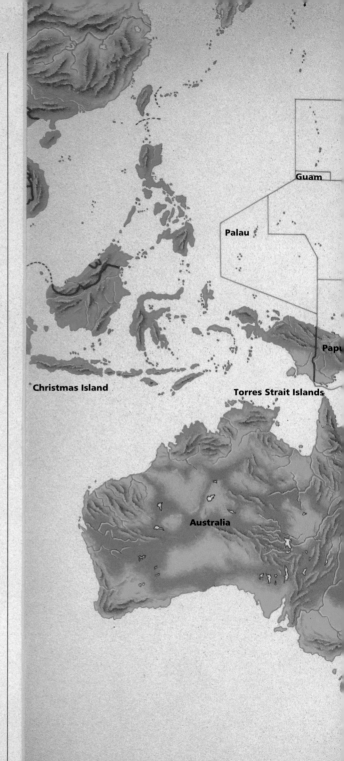

Guam

Palau

Papu

Christmas Island

Torres Strait Islands

Australia

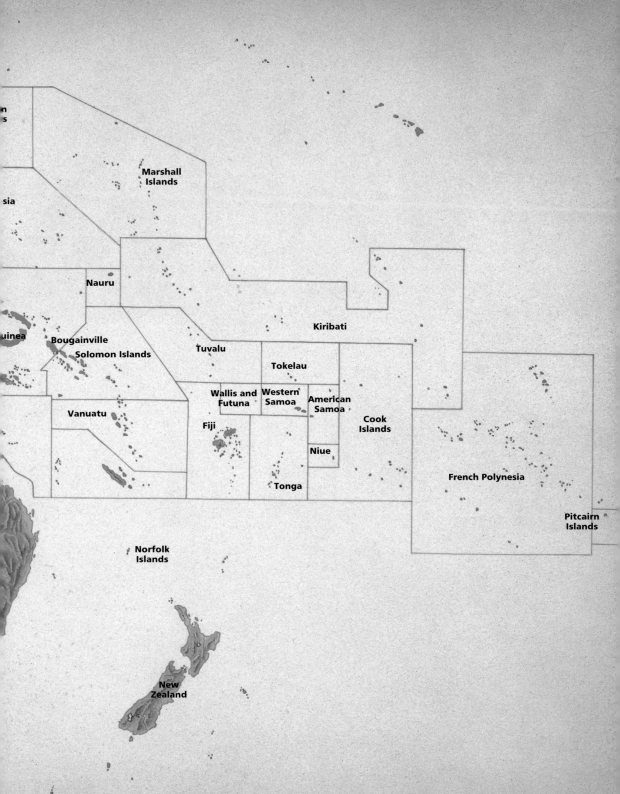

n
s

sia

Marshall
Islands

Nauru

uinea

Bougainville
Solomon Islands

Tuvalu

Kiribati

Tokelau

Wallis and
Futuna

Western
Samoa

American
Samoa

Vanuatu

Fiji

Cook
Islands

Niue

French Polynesia

Tonga

Pitcairn
Islands

Norfolk
Islands

New
Zealand

AUSTRALIA

CHRISTMAS ISLAND

Territory of Christmas Island
Autonomous external territory of Australia in
E Indian Ocean.

NATIONAL FLAG

Introduced in 1987. Proportions 1:2.

The yellow and green, the national colours
of Australia, and the stars of the Southern
Cross constellation symbolize the island's
association with Australia. The blue stands
for the Indian Ocean, the green for the
tropical rainforest and the bird is a golden
bosun, unique to the island. A graphic
representation of the island appears on the
yellow disc in the centre of the flag.

TORRES STRAIT ISLANDS

Part of Queensland (Australia)
with limited autonomy.

NATIONAL FLAG AND CIVIL ENSIGN

Introduced in May 1992. Proportions 23:31.

The traditional *dhari* headdress symbolizes
the inhabitants of the islands, which are
represented by the star. The green stands for
the land, the blue for the sea and the black
for the indigenous people.

AUSTRALIA

Commonwealth of Australia.
Federal constitutional monarchy comprising the
continent of Australia.

NATIONAL FLAG

*Introduced in 1901, approved by the
King of Great Britain in 1903. Proportions 1:2.*

The British blue ensign, charged with five
stars forming the Southern Cross and a
sixth to represent the Commonwealth of
Australia, was the design chosen in a
competition in 1901, which attracted
30,000 entries. Subsequently there were
some changes to the stars until their shape,
size and position were precisely specified
on 15 April 1954. The six points of the
Star of the Commonwealth represent the
six states, and the seventh stands for the
Northern Territory and the six external
territories of Australia.

THE SOUTHERN CROSS

The crux is the most distinctive
constellation of the Southern
Hemisphere. It is visible in the night
skies from south of about 30°N
latitude. Of the main four stars the
largest is the bottom one, the double
star acrux, and the brightest is the star
on the left, the *Alpha crucis*. This bright
constellation was used as a navigational
aid by the islanders in Oceania and by
the European discoverers. It became a
popular emblem among the settlers,
and since the 19th century has been
displayed on many flags in the
Southern Hemisphere.

AUSTRALIAN STATES AND TERRITORY

The state flags follow the design of the
British colonial flags, i.e. the blue ensign
in proportions 1:2, charged with a badge.
Almost all of them are older than the
national flag of Australia.

NEW SOUTH WALES

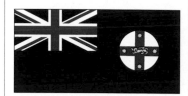

STATE FLAG

Granted 11 July 1876.

The cross of St George is charged with
the English lion and the four stars of the
Southern Cross.

NORTHERN TERRITORY

FLAG OF THE TERRITORY

Adopted 1 July 1978.

Black and ochre are the official colours of
the Territory. The stars form the Southern
Cross constellation. The seven petals of
the highly stylized Sturt's desert rose
(*Gossypium sturtianum*) and the seven-
pointed star in its centre represent the
seven states-to-be of Australia.

QUEENSLAND

STATE FLAG

Granted 29 November 1876.

The badge displays a blue Maltese cross surmounted by a royal crown. The shape of the cross resembles the insignia of the military award for valour, known as the Victoria Cross.

SOUTH AUSTRALIA

STATE FLAG

Adopted 13 January 1904.

The golden disc, which symbolizes the rising sun, is charged with a black and white piping shrike (*Gymnorhina tibicen hypoleuca*) perched on the branch of a gum tree. The piping shrike, or white-backed magpie, is the South Australian bird emblem.

TASMANIA

STATE FLAG

Adopted 25 September 1876.

The badge on Tasmania's flag is white with a heraldic lion in red. The same red lion appears in the crest of the Tasmanian coat of arms and the arms of the city of Hobart.

VICTORIA

STATE FLAG

Adopted 30 November 1877.

The flag of Victoria is the only state flag that does not bear a badge. Since 1870 it has been charged with the five stars of the constellation of the Southern Cross. The Tudor crown was added in 1877 and originally signified the state's ties to Queen Victoria and Britain. In 1952 it was replaced by St Edward's crown.

WESTERN AUSTRALIA

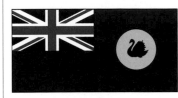

STATE FLAG

Adopted in 1953.

As early as 1830, a black swan (*Cygnus atratus*) became the emblem of the colony, which was also known as "the Swan River Colony". Aboriginal legend tells how the ancestors of a section of the Bibbulman tribe of western Australia were originally black swans who changed into men.

The badge, introduced on 27 November 1875, was yellow with the black swan turned out to the fly; in 1953 a mirror image of this was introduced instead.

THE CHANGING STARS

The first recorded attempt to adopt the national flag of Australia occurred in 1824 when Captain John Bingle and Captain John Nicholson charged the British white ensign with four stars. Each of the white eight-pointed stars was placed in the middle of each arm of the St George's cross.

In 1831, Captain J. Nicholson introduced a New South Wales ensign of very similar design. The colour of the cross was changed to dark blue and the fifth star was positioned in the centre of the cross. This flag became very popular in Australia and in the 1880s and 1890s was the chief symbol of the political movement towards the federation of Australian territories.

The first national flag of Australia was hoisted for the first time on 3 September 1901. It was the British blue ensign charged with a large star underneath the canton and five stars forming the constellation of the Southern Cross in the fly. The larger star, called the Commonwealth Star, had six points representing the six states of the new nation. The five stars in the fly had nine, eight, seven, six and five points, reflecting the brightness of the Southern Cross. In 1903, after minor modification, this flag became the current national flag of Australia.

In the last two decades there were several attempts to design and introduce a new national flag without the Union Jack in the canton. It is quite probable that in the near future Australia will have a new flag and it is almost certain that any new design will incorporate the stars of the Southern Cross.

WEST PACIFIC OCEAN

PAPUA NEW GUINEA

**Independent State of
Papua New Guinea**, Pidgin **Papua Niugini**.
Constitutional monarchy in E part of
New Guinea, W Pacific Ocean.

NATIONAL FLAG, STATE AND CIVIL ENSIGN

Approved 11 March 1971. Proportions 3:4.

Young student Susan Hareho Karike,
designer of the flag, chose red and black
because of the widespread use of these
colours in traditional native art. The
Empress of Germany's bird of paradise
(*Paradisaea raggiana augustae-victoriae*) is
peculiar to the island of New Guinea. The
five stars form the constellation of the
Southern Cross, symbolizing the
relationship with Australia and also
referring to a local legend about five sisters.
   The flag was only for use on land from
1971 to 16 September 1975, when the
country became independent.

BOUGAINVILLE

Republic of Bougainville.
Secessionist province of Papua New Guinea
in W Pacific Ocean.

NATIONAL FLAG

Introduced 1 September 1975. Proportions 1:2.

When the province of North Solomons
broke ties with Papua New Guinea in
May 1990 and proclaimed independence
under the name of Bougainville, its flag
remained unchanged. The blue background
symbolizes the Pacific Ocean surrounding
Bougainville, which is represented by the
centrally positioned emblem. The black
disc recalls the native Bougainvillean
people. In its centre is an *upe*, the headdress associated with the transition of
young men from adolescence to manhood.
The red stripes on the *upe* generally suggest
leadership. A broad central stripe and two
narrower lateral stripes represent men and
women, since for ceremonial occasions all
men paint the centre of their hair red,
whilst the women decorate the sides of their
hair red and leave the centre black. The disc
is framed by a green ring representing the
island. The white triangles allude to the
carved turtle shells worn by local chiefs and
their queens on ceremonial occasions.

SOLOMON ISLANDS

Constitutional monarchy comprising a group
of islands in SW Pacific Ocean.

NATIONAL FLAG

Adopted 18 November 1977. Proportions 1:2.

The stars originally represented the five
districts of the country, but in 1982 when
the country was divided into seven
provinces, it was decided that the stars
would instead symbolize the five main
groups of islands. The yellow stands for the
sun, the blue for water (the sea, rivers and
the rain) and the green for land, its trees
and food crops.

VANUATU

Republic of Vanuatu,
Bislama **Ripablik blong Vanuatu**.
Republic comprising a group of islands
in SW Pacific Ocean.

NATIONAL FLAG AND ENSIGN

*Officially hoisted 30 July 1980.
Proportions 11:18.*

The national emblem consists of two
crossed *namele* leaves (*Phoenix sylvestris*)
surrounded by a boar's tusk. The leaves
symbolize peace and their 39 fronds
represent the 39 members of the
Representative Assembly. The boar's tusk is
a symbol of prosperity. The black represents
the people and the rich soil, the yellow
(shaped like the archipelago) symbolizes
peace and the light of Christianity, the
green represents the islands and the red is a
symbol of the unity of the Vanuatu people.

NAURU

Republic of Nauru, Nauruan **Naoero**.
Republic comprising an island in
W Central Pacific Ocean.

NATIONAL FLAG AND ENSIGN

Adopted 31 January 1968. Proportions 1:2.

The blue stands for the Pacific Ocean and
blue skies. The yellow line stands for the
Equator and immediately below it lies

the island, represented by a white star. Its 12 points symbolize the 12 original tribes of Nauru.

MICRONESIA

Federated States of Micronesia.
Federal republic comprising most islands of the Caroline group in N Pacific Ocean.

NATIONAL FLAG AND ENSIGN

Adopted 30 November 1978. Proportions 1:2.

The blue represents the Pacific Ocean. The stars stand for the groups of islands forming the Federation.

MICRONESIAN STATES

Since 1947 the Caroline Islands (Chuuk, Kosrae, Palau, Pohnpei and Yap) have been administered by the USA as part of the United Nations Trust Territory of the Pacific Islands. Palau did not join the Federated States of Micronesia created in 1979.

Although some of the four constituent states have established proportions for their flags, the flags are manufactured in the United States in the standard proportions of 2:3 and 3:5.

CHUUK

Adopted 7 September 1979, approved 28 January 1980.

The blue stands for peace. The 38 stars represent the 38 municipalities and the coconut tree in the centre is a symbol of the local agriculture.

KOSRAE

Adopted 30 July 1981.

The blue represents the Pacific Ocean. The *fafa* pounding stone symbolizes local culture, custom, knowledge and prosperity. The olive branches denote peace and unity among the state and municipal government and the people. The four stars stand for the four main municipalities.

POHNPEI

Adopted in December 1977.

The half coconut shell represents the *sakau* cup. (*Sakau* is a local drink extracted from kava roots and hibiscus bark, and used during traditional ceremonies.) The stars represent the municipalities. The coconut branches signify the people's dependence on coconut resources.

YAP

Adopted 30 May 1980, officially hoisted 1 March 1981.

The blue stands for the Pacific Ocean, the white for peace and brotherhood. The highly stylized outrigger canoe is a symbol of the means and ways of accomplishment. The large circle symbolizes unity, while the smaller one represents the state and the people. The star is symbolic of guidance and the state's goals.

PALAU

Republic of Palau, Palauan **Belau.**
Federal republic comprising a group of islands in NW Pacific Ocean.

NATIONAL FLAG AND ENSIGN

Adopted 13 June 1980. Proportions 3:5.

The blue stands for the final transition from foreign domination to independence. The disc in the centre represents the full moon, which is the time for fishing, cutting trees, canoe-carving, planting, harvesting and celebrating.

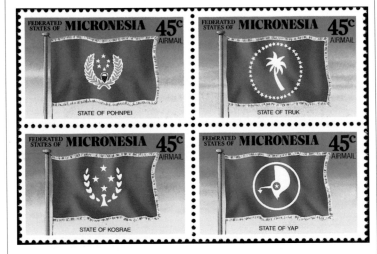

ABOVE
State flags on Micronesian postage stamps: (*clockwise from top left*) Pohnpei; Truk (Chuuk); Kosrae; Yap.

GUAM

Territory of Guam.
Unincorporated United States territory comprising the largest of the Mariana Islands in NW Pacific Ocean.

CIVIL AND STATE FLAG

Approved 9 February 1948. Proportions 22:41.

The basic design of the flag was approved on 4 July 1917, and in 1948 a narrow red border was added. The blue stands for the Pacific Ocean. The seal is in the shape of a sling-shot used by the ancient Chamorros for hunting and warfare. It is a symbol of the protection and endurance of the home government. The seal depicts a typical landscape in Guam, seen from the mouth of the Agana River. The lonely coconut palm tree escaped being uprooted during the destructive typhoon of 1918 and

therefore it symbolizes perseverance, courage, strength and usefulness (coconut is the main crop of the island). In the distance is "Two Lovers' Point" which represents faithfulness to a good cause. According to legend, two lovers preferred to kill themselves by jumping from the Point rather than be forced to marry someone they did not love. The outrigger canoe recalls the fame of the native people, the Chamorros, for their nautical skills. It stands for bravery and skill in making the best of one's environment.

NORTHERN MARIANAS

Commonwealth of the Northern Mariana Islands.
Self-governing incorporated United States territory in NW Pacific Ocean.

NATIONAL FLAG AND ENSIGN

Introduced 1 July 1989. Proportions 20:39 (de facto 2:3 or 3:5).

The first flag, adopted in 1972 and introduced in 1976, was blue with a large white star in the centre, superimposed over a grey *latte* stone in silhouette (*latte* stones, columns of limestone, were used to support traditional houses). In 1989 the emblem was surrounded with a garland of flowers and shells. It underwent some modification in 1991 and 1995.

The blue symbolizes the Pacific Ocean, which surrounds the islands with love and peace, and the star represents the Commonwealth. The *latte* stone symbolizes the culture of the Chamorro people. The circular head wreath made from four flowers (*ylang-ylang, seyur, ang'gha* and *teibwo*) is a symbol of the indigenous Carolinian culture.

CENTRAL PACIFIC OCEAN

KIRIBATI

Republic of Kiribati.
Republic comprising three groups of islands in E Central Pacific Ocean.

NATIONAL FLAG AND ENSIGN

Officially hoisted 12 July 1979. Proportions 1:2.

This is the heraldic banner of arms of Kiribati. The frigate bird (*Fregata minor*) is a symbol of authority, freedom and traditional dances. The rising sun stands for the Equator, whose length within the borders of Kiribati is more than 4000 km (2500 miles). The white and blue waves symbolize the Pacific Ocean, of which some 5 million sq km (2 million sq miles) belong to Kiribati.

TOKELAU

Overseas territory of New Zealand comprising a group of islands in Central Pacific Ocean.

NATIONAL FLAG

Adopted in October 1986. Proportions 1:2.

The blue represents the Pacific Ocean. The silhouette of a palm tree represents the local flora and the three stars stand for the atolls of Atafu, Fakaofo and Nukunonu.

AMERICAN SAMOA

Territory of American Samoa.
Self-governing United States overseas territory in Central Pacific Ocean.

CIVIL AND STATE FLAG

Adopted 27 April 1960. Proportions 1:2.

The colours are those of the United States flag, the *Stars and Stripes*. The American bald eagle, a symbol of protection, is holding in its talons a *fue*, or fly switch, the Samoan chief's attribute and a symbol of wisdom, and a *nifo oti*, a Samoan dancing knife. The fact that the eagle holds these symbols of Samoan authority and culture indicates the friendship between Samoan and American people.

SAMOA

Independent State of Samoa,
Samoan **Malotutu'atasi o Samoa i Sisifo**.
Constitutional monarchy in Central Pacific Ocean.

NATIONAL FLAG AND ENSIGN

Adopted 26 April 1949. Proportions 1:2.

On 26 May 1948, before adoption of the current flag, a similar flag with four stars was approved for use on land only. The five stars represent the constellation of the Southern Cross. The colours represent the qualities of freedom (blue), purity (white) and courage (red).

WALLIS AND FUTUNA

French **Territoire des Îles Wallis et Futuna**.
Autonomous French overseas territory in Central Pacific Ocean.

NATIONAL FLAG AND CIVIL ENSIGN

Introduced in 1888.

Originally a red flag with a white cross pattée was used in the 19th century in Uvea. The cross was introduced by the first Marist Brothers, the French missionaries who established the missions. When, in 1886, the Queen of Wallis accepted the French Protectorate it was agreed to charge the canton with the French *Tricolore*.

TUVALU

South West Pacific State of Tuvalu.
Constitutional monarchy comprising an island group in Central Pacific Ocean.

NATIONAL FLAG AND ENSIGN

Officially hoisted 1 October 1978, re-established 11 April 1997. Proportions 1:2.

The British blue ensign, with the field changed to light blue, is charged with nine yellow stars, representing the nine islands of the nation (Nanumea, Niutao, Nanumanga, Nui, Vaitupu, Nukufetau, Funafuti, Nukulaelae and Niulakita). The arrangement of the stars reflects the positions of the islands on the map, oriented to the east (east is at the top of the flag instead of north).

MARSHALL ISLANDS

Republic of the Marshall Islands,
Marshallese **Republic eo an Aelon in Majel**.
Republic consisting of two chains of islands in NW Pacific Ocean.

NATIONAL FLAG AND ENSIGN

Officially hoisted 1 May 1979. Proportions 10:19.

The blue stands for the Pacific Ocean. The star represents the nation, and its 24 points stand for the 24 municipalities. The four longer rays stand for Majuro (the capital), Wotji, Jaluit and Kwajalein. These rays form a cross, the symbol of the Christian faith of the islanders. The position of the star reflects the geographical position of the Marshall Islands a few degrees north of the Equator, which is represented by two stripes. Their shape (widening to the fly) symbolizes the increase in growth and vitality of life. The orange stands for wealth and bravery, the white for brightness.

FIJI

Republic of Fiji.

Republic comprising a group of islands
in S Pacific Ocean.

NATIONAL FLAG

*Officially hoisted 10 October 1970.
Proportions 1:2.*

For the first time in history, the colour of
the blue ensign was changed to distinguish
this flag from the flags of Australia and
New Zealand. The light blue symbolizes the
Pacific Ocean. The central device on the
shield of arms, granted in 1908, is the cross
of St George separating local agricultural
products (sugar cane, coconuts and
bananas) and a flying dove with a breadfruit
leaf in its beak, the emblem of the
Kingdom of Fiji (1871–1874). On the
upper part of the shield is a British lion
holding a coconut between its paws.

TONGA

Kingdom of Tonga.

Constitutional monarchy in S Pacific Ocean.

NATIONAL FLAG, CIVIL AND STATE ENSIGN

Adopted 4 November 1875. Proportions 1:2.

The flag reflects the deep-rooted
Christianity in Tonga. The cross reminds
the people that they owe their salvation to
the sacrifice made by Jesus on the Cross,
the red represents the blood Jesus shed
and the white stands for purity.

OCEANIA

For many years Oceanic societies did not
use flags and only some of them used
vexilloids. This began to change, however,
when the Europeans discovered this area
of the world, bringing their influences
with them. The Spanish first explored the
Pacific Ocean in the 16th century, the
Dutch in the 17th and the British in the
18th. The French were the first to establish
a protectorate in Polynesia, followed by the
Germans in Samoa and then the British and
the Americans. Most of the French colonies
had their own flags and the British had
state ensigns and governor's flags. Most
American colonies have only adopted their
own flags in the last few decades.

Looking at the flags of this area can be a
history lesson in itself. Many flags from the
colonial period represented the developing
relationship between the colony and its
founding country. The historic flag of the
governor of the German colonies, for
instance, closely followed the German
national flag of that time. Other flags
clearly still show their colonial roots in the
chosen design and colours of their modern
flags and ensigns. Rimatara and Tongatapu
are part of the family of flags that display
the Christian cross; the Gilbert and Ellice
Islands and the Soloman islands are based
on the British Union Jack, and Tahiti,
Raiatea and Rimatara show influences from
the French Tricolore. Many flags from the
Pacific Islands have adopted the United
Nations blue as this colour also symbolizes
the Pacific Ocean.

The royal flag of Tonga is the oldest
example of an armorial banner used as the
flag of a head of state and dates from
1862; it is still in use today. Tonga's war
ensign is also clearly based on the British
white ensign.

NIUE

Associated State of New Zealand, an island
in S Pacific Ocean.

NATIONAL FLAG

Adopted in 1975. Proportions 1:2.

The larger star stands for Niue, the smaller
ones symbolize links with New Zealand.
The Union flag recalls the protectorate
Great Britain established in 1899 following
a request made by the kings and chiefs of
Niue. The golden yellow symbolizes "the
bright sunshine of Niue and the warm
feelings of the Niuean people toward New
Zealand and her people".

COOK ISLANDS

Associated State of New Zealand, a group
of islands in S Pacific Ocean.

NATIONAL FLAG

*Officially hoisted 4 August 1979.
Proportions 1:2.*

The British blue ensign stands for links
with New Zealand. The 15 stars represent
the 15 islands. The stars symbolize heaven,
faith in God and the power that has
guided the inhabitants of the islands
throughout their history. The circle stands
for unity and strength.

SOUTH-WEST PACIFIC OCEAN

NORFOLK ISLANDS

Territory of Norfolk Islands.

External territory of Australia with full internal autonomy, SW Pacific Ocean.

NATIONAL FLAG

Adopted 11 January 1980.
Official proportions 1:2.

The central emblem of the flag is a Norfolk Island pine (*Araucaria heterophylla*). It appeared on the official seal for the first time in 1856.

NEW ZEALAND

Dominion of New Zealand.

Constitutional monarchy consisting of several islands in SW Pacific Ocean.

NATIONAL FLAG AND STATE ENSIGN

Adopted 12 June 1902. Proportions 1:2.

On 23 October 1869 this flag was adopted as the ensign of government vessels, and from 1902 it has also been the civil and state flag. The fly is charged with the four main stars of the Southern Cross constellation.

MAORI FLAGS

The native inhabitants of New Zealand adopted their first flag in 1857 when they chose their *kingi* (king) of *Niu Tireni* (New Zealand). Actually, there were three flags hoisted jointly one above another. The upper and the lower flags were long red rectangles with a white hoist portion charged with the red cross and three white squares with a red cross. In the middle was a red triangular flag with three white squares charged with a red cross.

More Maori flags appeared in the 1860s during the war against the colonists who were taking Maori land. The main feature of these flags was a red cross.

SOUTH-EAST PACIFIC OCEAN

FRENCH POLYNESIA

French **Territoire d'outre-mer de la Polynésie Française.**

Autonomous French overseas territory in SE Pacific Ocean.

NATIONAL FLAG

Adopted 23 November 1984. Proportions 2:3.

The red-white-red horizontal stripes recall the second national flag of the kingdom of Tahiti which was used from 1829 to 1847. The same flag with the addition of a French *Tricolore* became the flag of the protectorate and was used until 1880. After World War II a version without the canton was in popular, but unofficial, use. In 1975, the authorities agreed to allow the flag to be used with a 1:2:1 ratio of stripes.

To distinguish the flag of French Polynesia from that of Tahiti, the emblem was placed in the centre. Its main feature is a *piragua*, which is a status symbol as well as an indispensable boat used for fishing and transportation. Polynesian society is often compared to a *piragua* and the figures in the *piragua* stand for the five parts of French Polynesia: the Windward Islands, the Leeward Islands, the Tuamotu Archipelago, the Austral Islands and the Marquesas Islands. The golden yellow rays symbolize the sun and light, and the blue and white waves represent the riches of the Pacific on which the people have always relied for their livelihood.

PITCAIRN ISLANDS

British colony in SE Pacific Ocean.

STATE FLAG

Adopted 2 April 1984. Proportions 1:2.

The fly of the British blue ensign is charged with the coat of arms, granted on 4 November 1969. The centrepieces are the Bible and the anchor of the ship the *Bounty*. The green triangle represents the rugged cliffs of the island, the blue stands for the sea. The wheelbarrow in the crest stands for the first settlers, while a miro plant represents the wood the islanders use for carving souvenirs for tourists.

Flags of the Americas

The current national flags of the countries of the Americas, from Greenland and Canada to Argentina and the islands of the South Atlantic, are illustrated and described in the following pages, together with their territories, states and provinces.

For ease of reference, the countries of this huge continent have been grouped into geographical areas. We begin in North America and move on through Central America and the West Indies and the Caribbean. Finally, we look at the flags of the countries of South America and the islands of the South Atlantic.

For each entry, the country or territory's name is given in its most easily recognized form and then in all its official languages. This is followed by a description of its political status and geographic position. The basic data for each flag contains the status of the flag, date of adoption, proportions, and the symbolic meaning.

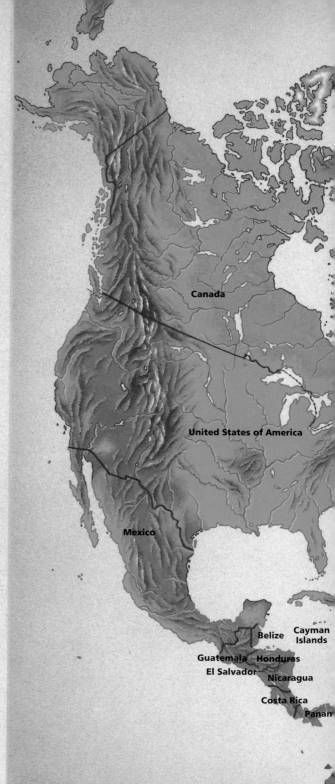

Canada

United States of America

Mexico

Belize

Cayman Islands

Guatemala   Honduras

El Salvador   Nicaragua

Costa Rica

Panam

Greenland

Venezuela

Guyana Surinam

Colombia

Ecuador

Peru

Bolivia Brazil

Paraguay

Chile

Saint-Pierre
et Miquelon

Argentina

Uruguay

Saint
Helena

Bermuda

The
Bahamas

Falkland
Islands

Dominican
Haiti Republic

South Georgia and
South Sandwich
Islands

Puerto
Rico Smaller islands of
the West Indies

Netherlands
Cuba Antilles Barbados

Trinidad and
Tobago

NORTH AMERICA

GREENLAND

Dan. **Grønland**,
nat. **Kalaallit Nunaat**.

Island NE of North America, outlying part
of Denmark with full self-government.

NATIONAL FLAG AND CIVIL ENSIGN.

Adopted 6 June 1985. Proportions 2:3.

The colours derive from the flag of
Denmark. The white stands for the ice
covering 83 per cent of the island, and the
red-white disc symbolizes the northern sun
with its lower half sunk in the sea.

CANADA

Federal constitutional monarchy in
N America.

NATIONAL FLAG AND ENSIGN

*Adopted 15 December 1964, officially hoisted
15 February 1965. Proportions 1:2.*

The maple leaf has been the symbol of
Canada since at least the middle of the
19th century. Red and white were approved
as the official colours of Canada in 1921.

CANADIAN PROVINCES
AND TERRITORIES

When the dominion of Canada was created
in 1867 there were only four provinces
(Ontario, Quebec, Nova Scotia and

New Brunswick). Today Canada comprises
ten provinces and two territories. Their
flags have different official proportions,
but in practice almost all are made and
displayed in the proportion 1:2.

ALBERTA

PROVINCIAL FLAG

*In use since 1967, officially approved
1 June 1968. Proportions 1:2.*

The blue field of the flag is charged with
the shield of arms, granted on 30 May 1907.
The shield displays the cross of St George
and a typical landscape in Alberta.

BRITISH COLUMBIA

PROVINCIAL FLAG

Adopted 20 June 1960. Proportions 3:5.

This banner of arms was granted on
31 March 1906. The Union Jack is a
reminder of British Columbia's origins as a
British colony and stands for its continued
links with the United Kingdom. The crown
represents the sovereign power that links,
in free association, the countries of the
Commonwealth. The sun setting over the
Pacific Ocean, symbolized by the wavy
stripes, reminds us that British Columbia
is the most westerly province of Canada.

MANITOBA

PROVINCIAL FLAG

Adopted 12 May 1966. Proportions 1:2.

The fly of the British red ensign is charged
with the shield of arms, granted on 10 May
1905. The shield displays the cross of
St George and a buffalo standing on a rock.

NEW BRUNSWICK

PROVINCIAL FLAG

Adopted 24 February 1965. Proportions 5:8.

This is the banner of arms, granted on
26 May 1868. The golden lion symbolizes
ties with the United Kingdom. The boat
signifies the importance of shipbuilding
and seafaring to the province.

NEWFOUNDLAND

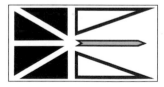

PROVINCIAL FLAG

Adopted 28 May 1980. Proportions 1:2.

The design is based on that of the British
Union flag. The colours symbolize snow and
ice (white), the sea (blue), human effort (red)
and confidence in the future (golden yellow).
The two red triangles represent the mainland
and island parts of the province. The arrow

stands for hope for the future. The trident (formed by the triangles and the arrow) refers to Newfoundland's continued dependence on fishing and the sea.

NOVA SCOTIA

PROVINCIAL FLAG

Officially approved 19 January 1929. Proportions 3:4.

This banner of arms was in use from 1625 to 1868, and was reinstated on 19 January 1929. The field shows the flag of Scotland in reversed colours. The shield displays the Royal Arms of Scotland.

ONTARIO

PROVINCIAL FLAG

Approved 21 May 1965. Proportions 1:2.

The fly of the British red ensign is charged with the shield of arms, granted on 26 May 1868. The shield displays the cross of St George and three maple leaves.

PRINCE EDWARD ISLAND

PROVINCIAL FLAG

Adopted 24 March 1964. Proportions 2:3.

The banner of arms was granted on 30 May 1905, having been used on the provincial Great Seal since 1769. The lion symbolizes ties with the United Kingdom. The larger tree is the oak of England and the tree saplings represent the three counties of the province. The green island reminds us that both Britain and the province are islands.

QUEBEC

PROVINCIAL FLAG

Adopted 21 January 1948. Proportions 2:3.

The white cross is taken from an ancient French military colour. The four fleurs-de-lis are based on the emblem of France under the reign of the Bourbons. The flag is called the *Fleurdelisé*.

SASKATCHEWAN

PROVINCIAL FLAG

Adopted 22 September 1969. Proportions 1:2.

The green represents the northern forested areas of the province and the yellow symbolizes the southern grainfield areas. The shield of arms, granted on 25 August 1906, appears in the upper hoist. The fly is charged with the western red lily, which is the floral emblem of the province.

NORTH-WEST TERRITORIES

FLAG OF THE TERRITORY

Adopted 1 January 1969. Proportions 1:2.

The blue vertical stripes represent the lakes and waters of the Territories and the white stands for the snow and ice. In the centre is the shield of arms, granted on 24 February 1956. The white symbolizes the polar icepack, the blue wavy stripe the North-west Passage, the green the forested areas and the red the tundra. The head of an arctic fox represents the local fauna. The yellow rectangles symbolize mineral riches.

YUKON

FLAG OF THE TERRITORY

Adopted 1 December 1967. Proportions 1:2.

The colours stand for the natural features of the province – the *taiga* forests (green), the winter snows (white) and the northern waters (blue). In the centre are the full arms adopted on 5 November 1956. The cross of St George stands for the first explorers and fur traders from England, the roundel of *vair* (heraldic fur) symbolizes the fur trade, the white and blue wavy lines symbolize the Yukon River and the rivers and creeks where gold was discovered, and the red triangles represent the mountains. The golden balls symbolize the territory's mineral resources, and the malamute dog, noted for its loyalty, stamina and courage, emphasizes the important role these animals played in the early history of the territory. Below the shield are two crossed branches of fireweed. This was adopted in 1956 as the floral emblem of Yukon.

SAINT-PIERRE ET MIQUELON

French **Collectivité territoriale des Îles Saint-Pierre et Miquelon**.
Dependency of France comprising two islands N of North America.

NATIONAL FLAG

This is a heraldic banner of arms. The blue is for the Atlantic Ocean and the ship commemorates French discoverer Jacques Cartier, who came to the islands in 1535. The emblems placed on the vertical stripe at the hoist are a reminder that the colonists came from the Basque Country (*ikkurina*), Brittany (ermine) and Normandy (two lions).

UNITED STATES

United States of America.
Federal republic in Central N America.

NATIONAL FLAG

Adopted 4 July 1960. Proportions 10:19.

The blue canton symbolizes the Union. The 50 stars stand for the 50 states. The 13 stripes represent the 13 colonies which formed the independent nation (New Hampshire, Massachusetts, Rhode Island, Connecticut, Delaware, Maryland, Virginia, North Carolina, South Carolina, Georgia, New York, New Jersey and Pennsylvania). The blue symbolizes loyalty, devotion, friendship, justice and truth; the red stands for courage, zeal and fervency; and the white represents purity and rectitude of conduct.

The *de jure* proportions of the national flag and the state flags are followed only by the government and the armed forces; the flags used by the general public are manufactured in the proportions of 2:3, 3:5 and 5:8.

AMERICAN STATES

The union formed in 1776 by 13 former British independent colonies has grown over the years, and since 1960 comprises 50 states and the federal District of Columbia. Most of the state flags displaying the arms or seal on a blue background are based on state military colours; some of them retain the proportions of these colours (26:33).

ALABAMA

STATE FLAG

Adopted 16 February 1895.
Official proportions 1:1, actual flags 2:3.

The red saltire stands for the most distinctive feature of the Confederate battle flag (a blue saltire with white stars).

ALASKA

STATE FLAG

Adopted 2 May 1927. Proportions 125:177.

This is the winning design in a flag contest. The blue represents the evening sky, the sea and mountain lakes, and the wild flowers that grow in Alaska. The golden yellow symbolizes the wealth that lies hidden in Alaska's hills and streams. The stars form the most conspicuous constellation in the northern sky, *Ursa major* (the Great Bear). The eighth star is Polaris, the North Star, "the ever-constant star for the mariner, explorer, hunter, trapper, prospector, woodsman and surveyor".

ARIZONA

STATE FLAG

Adopted 27 February 1917. Proportions 2:3.

Blue and gold are the colours of Arizona and the flag represents the copper star of Arizona rising from a blue field in front of the setting sun; mining is the most important industry of Arizona and copper is its main product. The red and yellow are the colours of Spain and are a reminder that the first whites to enter Arizona in 1540 were the Spanish *conquistadores*, headed by Coronado.

ARKANSAS

STATE FLAG

Adopted 10 April 1924. Proportions not specified.

The colours of the flag are those of both the United States and the Confederate States of America. The 25 white stars record that Arkansas was the 25th state admitted to the Union. The diamond shape indicates that Arkansas was the only diamond producing state of the Union, and the star above the name of the state commemorates the Confederacy. The other blue stars have a double meaning: they represent Spain, France and the United States, to which Arkansas successively belonged, and note that Arkansas was the third state formed out of the Louisiana Purchase.

CALIFORNIA

STATE FLAG

Adopted 3 February 1911. Proportions 2:3.

The design is based on the flag hoisted in Sonoma on 14 June 1846 when a group of Americans proclaimed an independent California republic. The grizzly bear is a symbol of strength.

COLORADO

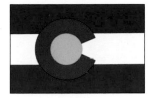

STATE FLAG

Adopted in 1911, officially approved 31 March 1964. Proportions 2:3.

The colours stand for the skies (blue), the gold (yellow), the mountain snows (white) and the soil (red). The capital "C" represents the name of the state.

CONNECTICUT

STATE FLAG

Introduced in 1895, adopted 3 June 1897. Proportions 26:33.

This is the design of the military colours from the Civil War period. The arms were granted on 25 October 1711. The three grapevines symbolize the three original settlements (Hartford, Windsor and Wethersfield), which formed the Colony of Connecticut in 1639. The motto means "He Who Transplanted Still Sustains".

DELAWARE

STATE FLAG

Adopted 24 July 1913. Proportions not specified.

The diamond stands for the state's nickname, the "Diamond State". The arms, adopted in 1777, indicate that the main industry is agriculture. The blue wavy stripe stands for the Delaware River. The ship in the crest recalls the fact that Delaware has access to the sea and to the benefits of commerce. The date recalls the day on which Delaware was the first state to ratify the Federal Constitution.

FLORIDA

STATE FLAG

Adopted 6 November 1900, seal modified in 1966 and 1985.

The red saltire is based on the battle flag of the Confederacy. The seal depicts a typical landscape in Florida, with an American Indian woman representing the original inhabitants of the peninsula.

GEORGIA

STATE FLAG

Adopted 13 February 1956 (effective 1 July 1956). Proportions 2:3.

The flag prominently displays the battle flag of the Confederacy and the state seal, with its tenets of wisdom, justice and moderation. The blue stands for reverence to God, loyalty, sincerity and justice; the white stands for purity; and the red for valour and sacrifice.

HAWAII

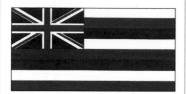

STATE FLAG

Adopted 20 May 1845. Proportions 1:2.

The flag is based on that adopted by the Kingdom of Hawaii in 1816. It combines the symbols of the United Kingdom (the Union Jack) and the United States (stripes of an early 19th-century ensign). The eight stripes represent the eight main islands: Hawaii, Kahoolawe, Kauai, Lanai, Maui, Molokai, Niihau and Oahu.

IDAHO

STATE FLAG

Introduced in 1907, formally adopted 15 March 1927. Proportions 26:33.

The female figure is a symbol of women's suffrage. She also represents liberty and justice, as denoted by the Phrygian cap (a symbol of liberty) and scales. The miner notes Idaho's chief occupation; the tree represents its timber interests; the ploughman and grain represent agriculture, and the cornucopias stand for horticulture. The elk's head refers to state game laws protecting elk and moose.

ILLINOIS

STATE FLAG

Basic design introduced in 1915. Proportions 3:5.

The bald eagle perched on an American shield indicates the allegiance of Illinois to the Union. The water stands for Lake Michigan. The name of the state was added on 1 July 1970.

INDIANA

STATE FLAG

Adopted 31 May 1917. Proportions 26:33.

The torch stands for liberty and enlightenment and the rays symbolize their far-reaching influence. The largest star represents Indiana, the 19th state of the Union. The outer circle of stars represents the original 13 states, and the inner circle of stars stands for the next five states admitted to the Union.

IOWA

STATE FLAG

Adopted 29 March 1921. Proportions 3:4.

The French *Tricolore* signifies ties with France before the Louisiana Purchase. The bald eagle denotes Iowa's allegiance to the Union; it holds in its beak a ribbon with the state motto "Our liberties we prize and our rights we will maintain".

KANSAS

STATE FLAG

Adopted 30 June 1963. Proportions 3:5.

This design, without the word "Kansas", was adopted on 23 March 1927. The sunflower is the state flower, the wreath symbolizes the Louisiana Purchase and the 34 stars record the fact that Kansas was the 34th state admitted to the Union. The state motto "To the stars through difficulties" reflects the political trials of Kansas prior to joining the Union. A man ploughing with horses represents agriculture as the basis of the future prosperity of the state, and the steamboat is a symbol of commerce. The past of Kansas is represented by a settler's cabin, a train of ox wagons going west and a herd of buffalo retreating, pursued by two native Americans on horseback.

KENTUCKY

STATE FLAG

Adopted 26 March 1918. Proportions 10:19.

The seal of the state was adopted in 1792. Above it appears the name of the state and below the seal are two crossed branches of golden rod, the state flower. The two friends embracing exemplify the state motto "United we stand, divided we fall".

LOUISIANA

STATE FLAG

Adopted 1 July 1912. Proportions 2:3.

The emblem is taken from the state seal, adopted in 1902. The pelican is the state emblem of Louisiana and is shown nourishing its young on blood from its own breast, signifying self-sacrifice. The scroll bears the state motto, "Union, Justice and Confidence".

MAINE

STATE FLAG

Adopted 24 February 1909. Proportions 26:33.

The state arms display a white pine (*Pinus strobus*), which stands for the state and its nickname "the Pine Tree State". The moose, native to Maine, is a symbol of large areas of unpolluted forests. The water symbolizes the sea. The farmer resting on a scythe represents the land and agriculture; the sailor resting on an anchor represents the sea, as well as commerce and fisheries. The star and the motto *Dirigo* (I direct) refer to the fact

that the North Star was a guiding star for sailors, trappers and settlers.

MARYLAND

STATE FLAG

Adopted 9 March 1904. Proportions 2:3.

This armorial banner is unique among the flags of the 50 states. It is derived from the arms of two English families, Calvert and Crossland. Sir George Calvert was granted arms in 1622. His sons founded Maryland in 1634 and to create the arms of Maryland they adopted the quarterly arms of Calvert with the arms of Crossland, which belonged to their grandmother's family.

MASSACHUSETTS

STATE FLAG

Adopted 18 March 1908. Proportions 3:5.

A Native American holding a bow and arrow is an old emblem of the colony, dating back to the first half of the 17th century. The star represents the Commonwealth of Massachusetts. The motto was adopted in 1775 by the provincial congress as a message for England, "By the sword we seek peace, but peace only under liberty". The crest (an arm with a sword) was added in 1780.

MICHIGAN

STATE FLAG

Adopted 1 August 1911. Proportions 2:3.

Since 1837 this has been a flag of the Michigan militia. The bald eagle represents the superior authority and jurisdiction of the United States; the elk and moose represent the local fauna. The word *Tuebor* ("I will defend") refers to Michigan's geographic position on the frontier. The sun rising over the lake calls attention to a man standing on a peninsula. His upraised right hand symbolizes peace but his left hand holds a rifle, indicating readiness to defend the state and the nation. On the scroll appears the state motto – "If you seek a pleasant peninsula look about you".

MINNESOTA

STATE FLAG

Adopted 19 March 1957. Proportions 3:5.

The 19 stars are because Minnesota was the 19th state to be admitted to the Union. The motto *L'Etoile du Nord* (the North Star) refers to the fact that Minnesota was once the northernmost state of the Union. The central scene displays a Native American giving way to a white settler.

MISSISSIPPI

STATE FLAG

Adopted 7 February 1894. Proportions 2:3.

The flag displays the national colours. The enlarged canton is charged with the battle flag of the Confederacy. The flag's features were specified on 6 September 1996.

MISSOURI

STATE FLAG

Adopted 23 March 1913. Proportions 7:12.

The 24 stars recall that Missouri was the 24th state to be admitted to the Union. The bears indicate the size and strength of the state. The national arms symbolize the allegiance of Missouri to the union and the crescent stands for a new state, the second to be carved from the Louisiana Purchase.

MONTANA

STATE FLAG

Introduced 1 July 1981.
Proportions 2:3, 3:5 or 5:8.

The basic design of the flag has been unchanged since 1905; the word "Montana" was added in 1981. The seal, dating from 1865, displays the Great Falls of Missouri and the Rocky Mountains. The plough, shovel and pick indicate the state's reliance on agriculture and mining.

NEBRASKA

STATE FLAG

Adopted 2 April 1925. Proportions unspecified.

The main natural features displayed on the seal are the Rocky Mountains and the Missouri River. The smith symbolizes the mechanical arts and agriculture is represented by shocks of grain, growing grain and a settler's cabin. The steamboat and train represent the role of transport.

NEVADA

STATE FLAG

Adopted 8 June 1991.
Proportions 2:3, 3:5 or 5:8.

The star symbolizes the state; its colour stands for silver, the main mineral product of Nevada. The state motto "Battle Born" is a reminder that Nevada was admitted to the Union during the Civil War. The emblem is flanked by two sprays of sagebrush which is the state flower.

NEW HAMPSHIRE

STATE FLAG

Adopted 1 January 1932.
Proportions unspecified.

The sun rises behind a broadside view of the frigate *Raleigh*, which was one of the first 13 vessels ordered for the American navy. It was built at Portsmouth in 1776, the year New Hampshire achieved independence. The nine stars refer to the fact that New Hampshire was the ninth state admitted to the Union.

NEW JERSEY

STATE FLAG

Adopted 26 March 1896.
Proportions unspecified.

Buff is the regimental colour of the New Jersey Continental Line, prescribed by General G. Washington in 1779. Buff became the colour of the field of state regimental colour in 1780. The main device of the arms is three ploughs, as New Jersey was the third state admitted to the Union. The figures of Liberty and Ceres (the goddess of agriculture) support the arms. The horse's head symbolizes vigour.

NEW MEXICO

STATE FLAG

Adopted 11 March 1925. Proportions 2:3.

The colours of the flag are those of Spain. The Zia sun symbol is that of the ancient Zia Pueblo Native Americans.

NEW YORK

STATE FLAG

Adopted 2 April 1901. Proportions 10:19.

The shield displays a landscape with the Hudson River and the rising sun symbolizes a bright future. It is supported by the figures of Liberty and Justice.

NORTH CAROLINA

STATE FLAG

Adopted 9 March 1885. Proportions 3:4.

The flag displays the national colours. The star and the letters "NC" symbolize the state. The dates recall two important documents from the era of the Revolution: the Mecklenburg Declaration of Independence and the Halifax Resolutions.

NORTH DAKOTA

STATE FLAG

Adopted 3 March 1911. Proportions 26:33.

The flag conforms in all respects to the regimental colours carried by the First North Dakota Infantry in the Spanish American War and the Philippine Insurrection, except for the name of the state on the scroll below the eagle.

OHIO

STATE FLAG

Adopted 9 May 1902. Proportions 8:13.

The flag displays the national colours. The white circle suggests the name "Ohio". The 17 stars signify that Ohio was the 17th state to enter the Union. The white circle with the red centre represents a buckeye (*Aesculus glabra*), the state tree, which gave the state its nickname, "the Buckeye State". The shape of the flag represents the hills and valleys of the state. The stripes symbolize the roads and waterways of Ohio.

OKLAHOMA

STATE FLAG

Adopted 9 May 1941. Proportions unspecified.

The blue symbolizes loyalty and devotion, the shield stands for protection, and the crossed olive branch and pipe of peace symbolize the desire for peace.

OREGON

STATE FLAG, OBVERSE

STATE FLAG, REVERSE

Adopted 26 February 1925. Proportions 500:833.

The arms are accompanied by the date of the state's admission to the Union. The 33 stars signify that Oregon was the 33rd state admitted to the Union and the American eagle represents protection. The shield shows the Pacific Ocean in the setting sun with two ships, the British departing and the Americans arriving. The covered wagon represents the settlers, the wheatsheaf and plough are symbols of agriculture, and the pick represents mining.

PENNSYLVANIA

STATE FLAG

Adopted 13 June 1907. Proportions 27:37.

The American eagle denotes allegiance to the Union. The ship, the plough and the three wheatsheaves were taken from the arms of the counties of Philadelphia, Chester and Sussex (which is now part of Delaware) respectively.

RHODE ISLAND

STATE FLAG

Adopted 19 May 1897. Proportions 29:33.

The anchor has the motto "Hope" below it and has appeared on the seals of Rhode Island since 1664. The 13 stars represent the 13 original states.

SOUTH CAROLINA

STATE FLAG

Adopted 28 January 1861.
Proportions unspecified.

The crescent refers to the badge with the inscription "Liberty or Death" worn on the caps of the soldiers of two regiments formed in South Carolina in 1775, who fought during the American Revolution. The palmetto tree is a symbol of victory, adopted in 1776 after the fort at Sullivan's Island, in Charleston harbour, defeated the British fleet. The fort was built out of palmetto tree trunks, which grow abundantly on Sullivan's Island.

SOUTH DAKOTA

STATE FLAG

Adopted 11 March 1963, modified 1 July 1992.
Proportions 3:5.

The sun alludes to the former nickname of the state, "the Sunshine State". Its new nickname, "the Mount Rushmore State", has featured since 1992 around the lower portion of the sun. The seal depicts a typical landscape, in which the ploughman symbolizes agriculture, the steamboat transportation, the smelting furnace the mining industry, the cattle dairy farming, and the trees lumbering.

TENNESSEE

STATE FLAG

Adopted 17 April 1905. Proportions 3:5.

The flag is in the national colours, which symbolize purity (white), lofty aims (blue)

and the fame of Tennessee (red). The three stars represent the three geographical divisions of the state. They also refer to the fact that Tennessee was the third state to join the Union after the original 13. The circle symbolizes unity.

TEXAS

STATE FLAG

Adopted 25 January 1839. Proportions 2:3.

The Lone Star flag was designed for the Republic of Texas, and was retained as the state flag after Texas joined the Union in 1845. The colours represent loyalty (blue), purity (white) and bravery (red).

UTAH

STATE FLAG

Adopted 11 March 1913.
Proportions unspecified.

The beehive represents industry, the main virtue of the first settlers, and the sego lily, the state flower, is a symbol of peace. The American eagle symbolizes protection and the flags denote Utah's support to the nation.

VERMONT

STATE FLAG

Adopted 1 June 1923. Proportions unspecified.

The pine tree is the traditional emblem of New England; the sheaves of wheat and the cow represent agriculture. The two crossed pine branches symbolize the pine sprigs worn at the Battle of Plattsburgh in 1814.

VIRGINIA

STATE FLAG

Adopted 30 April 1861. Proportions unspecified.

Sic Semper Tyrannis ("Thus Ever to Tyrants") is the message of the Virginian seal. Virtus, the symbol of the Commonwealth, is dressed as an Amazon with her foot on Tyranny, represented by the prostrate body of a man holding a broken chain and a scourge in his hands.

WASHINGTON

STATE FLAG

Adopted 7 June 1923.
Proportions 2:3, 3:5 or 5:8.

The green reflects the state's nickname, "the Evergreen State". The present design of the seal, with the vignette of General George Washington, was adopted in 1967. It is an improved version of the seal which was adopted in 1889 when Washington became a state of the Union.

WEST VIRGINIA

STATE FLAG

Adopted 7 March 1929. Proportions 10:19.

The white is for the purity of the state institutions; the blue stands for the Union. The rock is a symbol of stability and continuity, and the date is the day the state was founded. The farmer and miner symbolize the two main industries, and the Phrygian cap (a symbol of liberty) and rifles indicate that the state won its freedom and will defend it by force of arms.

WISCONSIN

STATE FLAG

Introduced 1 June 1981. Proportions 2:3.

The blue flag with the arms was adopted on 29 April 1913. In 1981 the word "Wisconsin" and the date "1848" (admission to the Union) were added. The shield of arms displays symbols of agriculture, mining, manufacture and navigation. The arms and motto of the United States symbolize the allegiance of the state to the Union, and the badger refers to its nickname, "the Badger State". The main branches of the economy, mining and agriculture, are represented by lead ore and a cornucopia. The sailor and the miner symbolize labour on water and on land.

WYOMING

STATE FLAG

Adopted 31 January 1917. Proportions 7:10.

The red symbolizes the Native Americans and the blood of the pioneers who gave their lives. The white is a symbol of purity and uprightness; the blue is the colour of the skies and distant mountains, and also a symbol of fidelity, justice and virility. The bison represents the local fauna while the seal on it symbolizes the custom of branding livestock. The woman holding a banner with the words "equal rights" symbolizes the political position of women in the state, and the men represent the livestock and mining industries. The lamps signify the light of knowledge.

DISTRICT OF COLUMBIA

FLAG OF THE DISTRICT

Adopted 15 October 1938. Proportions 10:19.

The state flag is the banner of arms of George Washington.

BERMUDA

British colony comprising a group of islands in the Atlantic Ocean, E of North America.

CIVIL FLAG AND ENSIGN

Introduced in 1915. Proportions 1:2.

Bermuda was the first British colony to fly the defaced red ensign. The fly is charged with the arms, granted on 4 October 1910. The British lion supports a shield portraying the wreck of the *Sea Venture*,

which in 1609 carried the first settlers and came to grief on a reef.

MEXICO

United States of Mexico,
Spanish **Estados Unidos Mexicanos**.
Federal republic S of North America.

NATIONAL FLAG AND ENSIGN

Adopted 17 August 1968. Proportions 4:7.

After Mexico achieved independence, it adopted on 2 November 1821 a flag based on the French *Tricolore*. The green-white-red flag was charged with the national emblem, a modern interpretation of an ancient Aztec symbol. According to Aztec legend, an eagle grasping a serpent in its claws and standing on a flowering nopal cactus growing from a rock in the middle of the Tenochtitlan Lake appeared on the site where the Aztecs decided to build their capital city in 1325. The emblem has changed its form several times, the last time in 1968.

Originally the colours symbolized independence (green), purity of religion (white) and striving for unity between the native races and the Spaniards (red). Today they stand for hope (green), purity (white) and religion (red).

CENTRAL AMERICA

BELIZE

Constitutional monarchy in Central America.

NATIONAL FLAG AND ENSIGN

*Officially hoisted 21 September 1981.
Proportions unspecified.*

Blue and red are the colours of the ruling and opposition parties respectively, and the 50 leaves in the wreath symbolize 1950, when the independence movement began. The arms retain the main features of the arms granted to British Honduras on 28 January 1907: sailors' and woodsmen's tools and a sailing ship. The tree behind the shield is a mahogany tree and supporting it are two men, denoting racial diversity. The motto means "Flourish in the Shade".

GUATEMALA

Republic of Guatemala,
Spanish **República de Guatemala**.
Republic in Central America.

STATE FLAG AND ENSIGN

*Decreed on 26 December 1997.
Proportions 5:8. National flag and ensign
are without arms.*

Guatemala, like the other four former members of the United Provinces of Central America, has retained the colours of the Federation's flag. The blue-white-blue vertical tricolour with the state emblem was introduced in 1871 and the form of the emblem was changed in 1968

and again in 1997. The blue stands for justice and steadfastness, and the white for purity and uprightness. The main device of the emblem is a quetzal, the national bird of Guatemala and a symbol of liberty. The inscription on the scroll, "Liberty 15 September 1821", is the date when Central America broke with Spain. The rifles symbolize the will of the people to defend freedom, the swords stand for justice and sovereignty, and the wreath is a symbol of victory. The latest change involved the spelling of the date of independence. Since December 1997 the inscription reads "15 de Septiembre" instead of "15 de Setiembre".

HONDURAS

Republic of Honduras,
Spanish **República de Honduras**.
Republic in Central America.

NATIONAL FLAG, CIVIL AND STATE ENSIGN

Adopted 16 February 1866. Proportions 1:2.

The flag is based on the flag of the United Provinces of Central America. The five stars refer to the members of the Federation: Costa Rica, El Salvador, Guatemala, Honduras and Nicaragua. The blue stands for the skies and brotherhood; the white for the desire for peace and purity of thoughts.

EL SALVADOR

Republic of El Salvador,
Spanish **República de El Savador.**
Republic in Central America.

STATE FLAG

Adopted 15 September 1912. Proportions 3:5. Civil flag is without arms. Civil ensign, an alternative civil flag and state flag and ensign are without arms, with the inscription "Dios, Union, Libertad" in gold letters on the white stripe.

The flag and the emblem are based on those of the United Provinces of Central America. The Masonic triangle symbolizes equality; its angles represent three branches of government: legislative, executive and judicial. The volcanoes stand for the five nations of Central America flanked by the Pacific and the Atlantic Oceans. Within the triangle are symbols of liberty (a Phrygian cap), the ideals of the people (golden rays) and peace (rainbow). The motto, "*Dios, Union, Libertad*" ("God, Unity, Liberty") reflects faith in God, harmony in the family and the independence of the people. The 14 clusters of leaves represent the number of departments of El Salvador.

NICARAGUA

Republic of Nicaragua,
Spanish **República de Nicaragua**.
Republic in Central America.

STATE FLAG

Adopted 4 September 1908. Proportions 3:5. The alternative civil flag is without emblem.

The flag is based on that of the United Provinces of Central America. The triangle is a symbol of equality. The five volcanoes represent the five nations of Central America flanked by the Atlantic and Pacific Oceans. The Phrygian cap is a symbol of liberty; the rainbow symbolizes peace.

COSTA RICA

Republic of Costa Rica,
Spanish **República de Costa Rica**.
Republic in Central America.

STATE FLAG AND ENSIGN

Adopted 13 June 1964. Proportions 3:5. Civil ensign is without emblem.

In 1848 the present design of the flag with five stripes was adopted. The red was added to obtain the colours of revolutionary France and the national emblem was positioned in the centre. The current design of the flag and the emblem were adopted in 1964. The seven stars represent the seven provinces of Costa Rica and the volcanoes denote the geographical position of Costa Rica between the Pacific and the Atlantic. The sun is a symbol of freedom and the ships symbolize commerce.

PANAMA

Republic of Panama,
Spanish **República de Panama**.
Republic in Central America.

NATIONAL FLAG AND ENSIGN

Introduced 3 November 1903, officially approved 4 June 1904. Proportions 2:3.

The blue and red are the colours of the main political parties (Conservatives and Liberals respectively) and the white denotes peace between them. The blue also symbolizes the Pacific Ocean and the Caribbean, and the red stands for the blood of those who lost their lives for their country. The blue star represents the civic virtues of purity and honesty, and the red star is a symbol of authority and law.

WEST INDIES AND THE CARIBBEAN

THE BAHAMAS

Commonwealth of the Bahamas.
Constitutional monarchy comprising a chain
of islands NW of West Indies.

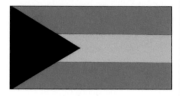

NATIONAL FLAG

Adopted 10 July 1973. Proportions 1:2.

The flag is a graphic representation of the
golden beaches of the Bahama Islands
surrounded by the aquamarine sea. The
black represents the vigour and force of a
united people. The triangle indicates the
enterprise and determination of the
Bahamian people to develop the rich
resources of land and sea.

TURKS AND CAICOS ISLANDS

British crown colony in the N Central West Indies.

STATE FLAG AND ENSIGN

Introduced in 1968. Proportions 1:2.
Civil ensign has a red field.

The fly is charged with the shield of arms,
granted on 26 September 1965. It displays
local flora and fauna: a queen conch shell,
a spiny lobster and a Turk's head cactus.

CUBA

Republic of Cuba,
Spanish **República de Cuba**.
Socialist republic comprising an island in
the W West Indies.

NATIONAL FLAG AND ENSIGN

Introduced in 1850, officially approved
20 May 1902. Proportions 1:2.

The flag was designed by a Cuban poet
Teurbe Tolón in 1849 and was patterned
on the design of the Stars and Stripes. The
star, called *La Estrella Solitaria* ("the Lone
Star"), was selected to light the way towards
freedom and was taken from the flag of
Texas. In time, the Cuban flag itself began
to be known as *La Estrella Solitaria*. The
flag was hoisted for the first time on
19 May 1850 in Ordenas on the north
coast of Cuba where General Francisco
Lopez landed with 600 men and staged
an abortive attempt to free the country
from colonial rule.

The triangle is a Masonic symbol of
liberty, equality and fraternity, and the
three blue stripes stand for the three
sectors into which Cuba was divided by
the Spaniards. The white symbolizes the
pure intentions of the revolutionaries and
for justice; the red is for the blood that was
shed in the struggle for independence.

CAYMAN ISLANDS

British colony in the W West Indies.

STATE FLAG AND ENSIGN

Introduced in 1958. Proportions 1:2.
Civil ensign has a red field.

The badge displays the whole achievement
of the arms, granted on 14 May 1958. The
three stars represent the three main islands:
Grand Cayman, Cayman Brac and Little
Cayman. The lion denotes loyalty to Great
Britain. A turtle and a pineapple represent
the fauna and flora of the islands.

JAMAICA

Constitutional monarchy comprising an island
in the W West Indies.

NATIONAL FLAG, STATE AND CIVIL ENSIGN

Officially hoisted 6 August 1962.
Proportions 1:2.

The green stands for hope and agriculture,
the black for hardships overcome and to be
faced, and the yellow for natural resources
and the beauty of sunlight.

HAITI

Republic of Haiti, French **République d'Haiti**.
Republic consisting of the W part of Hispaniola Island in the Central West Indies.

STATE FLAG

Introduced in 1897, re-introduced 25 February 1986. Proportions 3:5. Civil flag and ensign are without arms.

The blue and red are taken from the French *Tricolore* and represent the union of blacks and mulattoes. The arms are composed of a cabbage palm surmounted by the Phrygian cap of liberty and ornamented with trophies (rifles, flags, hatchets, cannons, cannonballs, trumpets, anchors etc). The motto means "Union Makes Strength".

DOMINICAN REPUBLIC

Spanish **República Dominicana**.
Republic consisting of the E part of Hispaniola Island in the Central West Indies.

STATE FLAG AND ENSIGN, WAR ENSIGN

*Adopted 6 November 1844.
Civil flag and ensign are without arms.
Proportions 5:8.*

In 1839 the Trinitarians struggling for independence added a white cross to the flag of Haiti to form their flag. Later the blue and red were reversed at the fly portion of the flag. The cross stands for the Catholic faith, the blue is the colour of liberty and the red symbolizes blood. The arms display the national colours and flags, the Cross and the Bible. The motto above the shield means "God, Fatherland, Liberty".

PUERTO RICO

Free Associated State of Puerto Rico,
Spanish **El Estado Libre y Asociado de Puerto Rico**.
Self-governing incorporated territory of the United States of America, an island in the Central West Indies.

NATIONAL FLAG

In use since 22 December 1895, official since 24 July 1952. Proportions 2:3.

The flag, designed in 1891, is that of Cuba with reversed colours. The star symbolizes the Fatherland. The triangle and the colours represent the republican ideals of liberty, equality and fraternity.

VIRGIN ISLANDS

Virgin Islands of the United States.
Organized, unincorporated territory of the United States of America comprising a group of islands in the E West Indies.

NATIONAL FLAG

Adopted 17 May 1921. Proportions unspecified.

The white is a symbol of purity. The emblem is a simplified version of the United States arms and the letters "V" and "I" stand for the Virgin Islands.

BRITISH VIRGIN ISLANDS

British colony in the E West Indies.

STATE FLAG AND ENSIGN

Proportions 1:2.

The arms, granted on 15 November 1960, appear in the centre of the British blue ensign. The central figure is St Ursula, the "wise virgin" and namesake of the islands. The eleven lamps represent the 11 virgins murdered with St Ursula by the Huns.

ANGUILLA

Dependency of the United Kingdom in the E West Indies.

STATE FLAG AND ENSIGN

Officially hoisted 30 May 1990. Proportions 1:2.

The British blue ensign is defaced with the shield of arms, which displays three dolphins, symbolizing unity and strength. The blue base stands for the Caribbean Sea surrounding the island.

ST KITTS AND NEVIS

Federation of St Kitts and Nevis.
Federal constitutional monarchy comprising
two islands in the E West Indies.

NATIONAL FLAG AND ENSIGN

Adopted 19 November 1983.
Proportions 2:3.

The two stars stand for hope and liberty,
and the black symbolizes the African
heritage of a major part of the population.
The green represents the fertility of the
land, the yellow the constant sunshine, and
the red symbolizes the struggle to end
slavery and colonialism.

MONTSERRAT

British crown colony consisting of a volcanic
island in the E West Indies.

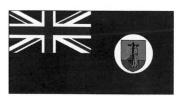

STATE FLAG AND ENSIGN

Adopted in 1960. Proportions 1:2.

The British blue ensign is defaced with the
arms, adopted in 1909. The cross stands for
Christianity. The woman with a harp refers
to the Irish immigrants who settled on the
island in 1632.

ANTIGUA AND BARBUDA

State of Antigua and Barbuda.
Constitutional monarchy comprising
three islands in the E West Indies.

NATIONAL FLAG AND ENSIGN

Introduced 27 February 1967. Proportions 2:3.

The sun symbolizes the new era of
independence in the history of the island.
The colours represent its African heritage
(black), hope (blue) and the dynamism of
the people (red). The "V" stands for victory.
The yellow, blue and white indicate the
country's main tourist attractions: the sun,
sea and sandy beaches.

DOMINICA

Commonwealth of Dominica.
Republic comprising an island in the E West Indies.

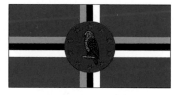

NATIONAL FLAG AND ENSIGN

Adopted 3 November 1990. Proportions 1:2.

The basic design of the flag was introduced
on 3 November 1978. Since then it has
undergone several modifications. The red
circle symbolizes socialism. The sisserou
parrot (*Psittacus imperialis*) is the national
bird, unique to Dominica, and symbolizes
flight towards greater heights and fulfilment
of aspirations. The ten stars represent the
ten parishes of equal status, thus the
equality of the people. The green

symbolizes the lush vegetation; the triple-
coloured cross represents the Trinity of God.
The yellow represents the sunshine, the
main agricultural products (citrus and
bananas) and the Carib people, the first
inhabitants of the island; the black is a
symbol of the rich black soil and African
heritage; the white symbolizes the rivers
and waterfalls, and purity of aspirations.

MARTINIQUE

French **Département de la Martinique.**
French overseas department and administrative
region, an island in the E West Indies.

NATIONAL FLAG

Adopted 4 August 1766. Proportions 2:3.

The flag is the old French merchant ensign
charged with four white serpents.

ST LUCIA

Constitutional monarchy consisting of an island
in the SE West Indies.

NATIONAL FLAG AND ENSIGN

Officially introduced 1 March 1967.
Proportions 1:2.

The triangle represents the twin peaks of
the Pitons, a geological formation of
volcanic origin. The black and white
symbolize the "two races living and working
in unity", the yellow symbolizes the

constant sunshine and the blue stands for the Caribbean and the Atlantic Ocean.

ST VINCENT AND THE GRENADINES

Constitutional monarchy comprising several islands in the SE West Indies.

NATIONAL FLAG AND ENSIGN

Officially hoisted 22 October 1985.
Proportions 2:3.

"The Gems", as the green lozenges and the flag itself are commonly called, is an abbreviation of "the Gems of the Antilles", which is the islands' nickname. They also represent the nature of the country, with numerous islands and peoples. The blue symbolizes the sky and the sea, and the green represents the lush vegetation and the vitality of the people. The yellow stands for the golden sands, the bright spirit of the people and warmth.

BARBADOS

Constitutional monarchy consisting of an island in the SE West Indies.

NATIONAL FLAG AND ENSIGN

Introduced 30 November 1966. Proportions 2:3.

The blue stands for the sea and the sky, and the yellow represents the sandy beaches.

The trident, an attribute of the mythical sea god Neptune, symbolizes some of the traditions of the past but the shaft is broken, indicating the break with the historical and constitutional ties of the past.

GRENADA

State of Grenada.
Constitutional monarchy comprising several islands in the SE West Indies.

CIVIL AND STATE FLAG

Officially hoisted 7 February 1974.
Proportions 3:5. Proportions of the ensign 1:2.

The yellow represents the sun and the friendliness of the people, the green stands for the agriculture and the red is a symbol of harmony, unity and courage. The seven stars represent the island's seven parishes. The nutmeg recalls that this small island is the second-largest producer of nutmeg in the world.

TRINIDAD AND TOBAGO

Republic of Trinidad and Tobago.
Republic of several islands in the S West Indies.

STATE FLAG

Officially hoisted 31 August 1962.
Proportions 3:5. Proportions of the ensign 1:2.

The black represents the dedication of the people, joined together by one strong

bond; it also symbolizes strength, unity, purpose and the wealth of the land. The red stands for the vitality of the people, the warmth and energy of the sun, and the courage and friendliness of the people. The white symbolizes the sea, purity of aspirations and the equality of all men under the sun.

NETHERLANDS ANTILLES

Dutch **De Nederlandse Antillen**.
Autonomous part of the Netherlands consisting of 5 islands in the E and S West Indies.

CIVIL AND STATE FLAG AND ENSIGN

Adopted 1 January 1986. Proportions 2:3.

The colours are based on those of the Netherlands flag. The blue represents the Caribbean and the stars stand for the five constituent parts of the Netherlands Antilles: Curaçao and Bonaire off the coast of Venezuela, St Maarten, St Eustatius and Saba in the Leeward Islands.

ISLANDS OF THE NETHERLANDS ANTILLES

The Netherlands Antilles are an integral part of the Netherlands realm. They consist of five islands: Curaçao, Bonaire, St Maarten, St Eustatius and Saba. St Eustatius does not have its own flag.

BONAIRE

FLAG OF THE ISLAND

Hoisted 15 December 1981. Proportions 2:3.

The star represents the island itself, while its six points recall the six neighbourhoods of Bonaire. The black ring around it, which represents a compass, symbolizes the seamanship of Bonaireans and their purposefulness in orienting themselves between the spirit (which is symbolized by the colour yellow) and the world (symbolized by the colour blue). The red is a symbol of energy, the blood of the people of Bonaire, and their struggle during their daily lives. The yellow stands for brilliant sunshine and the beauty of nature, especially the yellow flowers of brasilia and *Kibrahacha* (axe-breaker) plants. The white symbolizes liberty, tranquillity and peace. The blue is for the sea which provides a basis for their livelihood.

CURAÇAO

FLAG OF THE ISLANDS

Adopted 2 July 1984. Proportions 2:3.

Two stars represent the islands of Curaçao and Klein Curaçao. They are also seen as a symbol of peace and happiness. The five points of each star recall the five continents from which people came and settled the islands. The blue stands for the loyalty of the people; the upper blue symbolizes the sky, the lower stripe the sea. The yellow stripe stands for the tropical sun and reflects the joyful character of the Curaçao population.

SABA

FLAG OF THE ISLAND

Adopted 6 December 1985. Proportions 2:3.

The star represents Saba. Its colour stands for the wealth of natural beauty found on the island and symbolizes hope for the future. The colours symbolize historical and political ties with the Netherlands and the Netherlands Antilles. In addition, the white stands for peace, friendship, purity and serenity; the red for unity, courage and determination. The blue represents the sea which has played a significant role in the survival of the people of Saba. Blue also symbolizes the heavens which remind the people of Saba of God Almighty who created the island.

ST MAARTEN

FLAG OF THE ISLAND

Adopted 13 June 1985. Proportions 2:3.

The colours are those of the flag of the Netherlands. The arms show an old courthouse, a bouquet of yellow sage (the national flower), and a silhouette of the monument honouring Dutch-French friendship and the unity of both parts of the island. The orange border symbolizes loyalty to the ruling Dutch house of Orange-Nassau. The crest is formed by a yellow disc which represents the sun, and a grey silhouette of a pelican in flight. The motto in Latin, "Semper Progrediens" means "Always Progressing".

ARUBA

Autonomous overseas territory of the Netherlands, an island in the S West Indies.

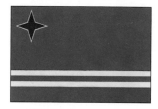

NATIONAL FLAG AND CIVIL ENSIGN

Officially hoisted 1 January 1986. Proportions 2:3.

The blue stands for the Caribbean and the skies. The star symbolizes Aruba, with its red soil and white beaches. The four points of the star represent the four major languages (Papiamento, Dutch, Spanish and English) and the four points of the compass, indicating that the inhabitants came from all over the world to live here in unity and strength. The stripes represent the sun and tourism, and the mineral resources of the island.

SOUTH AMERICA

COLOMBIA

Republic of Colombia,
Spanish **República de Colombia**.
Republic in NW South America.

CIVIL ENSIGN SINCE 1890

Adopted 26 November 1861. Proportions 2:3.
National flag and state ensign are
without the emblem.

The colours symbolize sovereignty and justice (yellow); nobility, loyalty and vigilance (blue); and valour, honour, generosity and victory achieved at the cost of bloodshed (red). According to another interpretation, the colours stand for universal liberty (yellow), the equality of all races and social classes before God and the law (blue), and fraternity (red).

VENEZUELA

Republic of Venezuela,
Spanish **República de Venezuela**.
Republic in NW South America.

STATE FLAG AND ENSIGN, WAR ENSIGN

Adopted 17 February 1954. Proportions 2:3.
Civil ensign is without arms.

This flag, with yellow, blue and red stripes of equal width, was introduced in 1836 and has since undergone several modifications in the arms and the arrangement of the stars. The seven stars represent the seven provinces that began the fight for independence. The emblems on the arms symbolize the unity of the 20 provinces (a wheatsheaf with 20 ears), the struggle for independence (flags and weapons) and liberty (a running horse). The cornucopias stand for the country's wealth and prosperity, and the wreath of laurel and palm is a symbol of glory and peace.

ECUADOR

Republic of Ecuador,
Spanish **República del Ecuador**.
Republic in NW South America.

STATE FLAG AND ENSIGN

Adopted 10 January 1861. Proportions 1:2.
Civil flag and ensign are without arms.

The colours of the flag represent the sunshine, grain and wealth (yellow), the sky, sea and rivers (blue), and the patriots and their blood shed in the struggle for freedom and justice (red). Mount Chimborazo and the river symbolize the ties between the interior of the country and the coastal areas; the steamship recalls the first South American steamship, built in 1841 in Guayaquil. The sun is a symbol of liberty and the signs of the zodiac denote the four memorable months (March-June) of the revolution in 1845. The condor is a symbol of strength and valour, and the *fasces* represents the sovereignty of the republic. The flags mounted on lances refer to the duty to defend the Fatherland with arms.

GUYANA

Co-operative Republic of Guyana.
Republic in N South America.

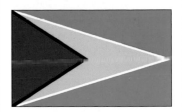

NATIONAL FLAG

Adopted 20 May 1966. Proportions 3:5.
Proportions of national ensign are 1:2.

Whitney Smith, the designer of the flag, chose green for the background because green forests and fields cover more than 90 per cent of Guyana. The red represents zeal and sacrifice, which are part of the nation-building process that the Guyanese are striving towards. The black border indicates the perseverance needed to reach their goal. The "golden arrowhead" represents the golden future the citizens hope will be built upon Guyana's mineral resources. The country's extensive water resources are symbolized by the white border.

SURINAM

Republic of Surinam,
Dutch **Republiek Surinam**.
Republic in N South America.

NATIONAL FLAG AND ENSIGN

Officially hoisted 25 November 1975.
Proportions 2:3.

The golden star is a symbol of the golden future that can be achieved through unity.

The green stands for the fertile land, the white for justice and freedom, and the red for progress in the struggle for a better life.

BRAZIL

Federative Republic of Brazil, Portuguese **República Federativa do Brasil**.

Federal republic in Central South America.

NATIONAL FLAG AND ENSIGN

Adopted 12 May 1992. Proportions 7:10.

The original design, with 21 stars, was adopted on 19 November 1889. The number of stars was increased to 22 in 1960, to 23 in 1968 and to 27 in 1992. The central device represents the sky above Rio de Janeiro at 8.30 a.m. on 15 November 1889, the date of the proclamation of the republic. The 27 stars correspond to the stars of the constellations of the Virgin, Water Snake, Scorpio, Southern Triangle, Octant, Southern Cross, Keel of Argo, Greater Dog and Smaller Dog. Each of 26 stars represents one state of the Federation and the 27th star represents the Federal District. The curved band with the national motto "Order and Progress" stands for the Equator. The green and yellow symbolize the forests and mineral resources respectively.

BRAZILIAN STATES

Since 1889 Brazil has been a federal republic. Currently it comprises 26 states and the federal district where Brasilia, the capital of the country, is located.

ACRE

STATE FLAG

Flag introduced in 1899, officially confirmed 1 March 1963. Proportions 11:20.

Yellow and green are the national colours of Brazil. The red stands for courage.

ALAGOAS

Adopted 23 September 1963. Proportions 4:7.

The colours are taken from the state arms, which display the arms of the cities of Alagoas, Penedo and Porto Calvo. The pictures of a stalk of sugar cane and a branch of cotton represent the state's two chief agricultural products.

AMAPÁ

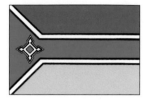

STATE FLAG

Adopted in 1984. Proportions 4:7.

The colours symbolize the sky and law (blue), the green land, faith in the future, freedom and love (green), the natural riches (yellow), purity and tranquillity (white), regard to the past being the source of good (black). The emblem represents the fort of São José de Macapá. The blue star stands for the state.

♦ **ABOVE** State flags on Brazilian postage stamps, 1981 (*from left to right beginning top right*) Alagoas; Bahia; Federal District; Pernambuco; Sergipe.

AMAZONAS

Flag introduced in 1897. Proportions 7:10.

The red stripe represents the state and the white stripes stand for the Amazon and Negro Rivers. The larger star symbolizes Manaus, the capital of the state, and the other stars represent the 43 other municipalities that form the state.

BAHIA

Flag adopted 26 May 1889. Proportions 7:10.

The red triangle represents the Masonic symbol of the *Inconfidencia Mineira*, the miners' revolt of 1789. Blue, white and red were the colours of the Bahian Revolution of 1798.

CEARÁ

Flag adopted 31 August 1967. Proportions 7:10.

Green and yellow are the national colours of Brazil. The central portion of the arms

displays the bay and lighthouse at Mucuri. The stars represent the municipalities of the state.

ESPIRITO SANTO

Flag officially hoisted 24 April 1947.
Proportions 7:10.

The colours of the flag represent peace (blue), harmony and sweetness (white), and joy (rose). The motto means "Work and Hope".

FEDERAL DISTRICT

Flag officially hoisted 7 September 1969.
Proportions 13:18.

The white stands for purity, and green and yellow are the national colours of Brazil. The four arrows symbolize the balance of centralization and devolution in Brazil.

GOIAS

Flag adopted 30 July 1919. Proportions 7:10.

The stars are those of the Southern Cross constellation. Green and yellow are the national colours of Brazil.

MARANHÃO

Adopted 21 December 1889. Proportions 2:3.

The white star stands for the state. The colours of the stripes represent the three components of the population: the descendants of the Portuguese discoverers and colonizers (white), the native Indians (red) and the African slaves.

MATO GROSSO

Flag adopted in 1890, officially confirmed 11 July 1947. Proportions 7:10.

The flag has the colours of the national flag but in a different arrangement. The star stands for the state.

MATO GROSSO DO SUL

Flag officially hoisted 1 January 1979.
Proportions 7:10.

The state is represented by a golden star shining in the blue sky of hope, symbolizing the wealth of the people's labour. The green stands for the forests and fields. The white band symbolizes the future and friendship among peoples.

MINAS GERAIS

Flag adopted 27 November 1962.
Proportions 7:10.

The triangle recalls the Inconfidencia Mineira, the miners' revolt of 1789.

◆ **ABOVE** State flags on Brazilian postage stamps, 1982 (*from left to right beginning top right*) Minas Gerais; Mato Grosso; Piaui; Maranhão; Santa Catarina.

PARÁ

STATE FLAG

Flag introduced 17 November 1889.
Proportions 7:10.

The star represents the state and the white symbolizes the river Amazon.

PARAÍBA

Flag introduced 27 October 1965.
Proportions 7:10.

The motto *Nego* ("I deny it") refers to the revolution of 1930, in which the state played a leading part.

PARANÁ

Flag officially adopted 31 March 1947.
Proportions 2:3.

The basic design of the flag was adopted in 1892. The green symbolizes the country's natural wealth, the white stands for its mineral resources. The main device of the emblem is the Southern Cross constellation. The branches of araucaria and maté represent forestry and agriculture.

PERNAMBUCO

Flag officially adopted 23 February 1917.
Proportions 2:3.

The flag was adopted by the republic of Pernambuco in 1817. The star represents the state, the three arches of the rainbow symbolize peace, friendship and union, and the sun signifies that the people of Pernambucos are the children of the sun. The cross refers to the name Santa Cruz (Holy Cross) which was given to Brazil by the European discoverers.

◆ **BELOW**
State flags on Brazilian postage stamps, 1983 (*from left to right beginning top right*) Amazonas; Goias; Rio de Janeiro; Mato Grosso Do Sul; Paraná.

PIAUÍ

Flag adopted 24 July 1922.
Proportions 7:10.

The star represents the state. The national colours of Brazil, yellow and green symbolize its allegiance to that country.

RIO DE JANEIRO

Flag introduced in 1947.
Proportions 7:10.

The flag displays the pre-1910 colours of Portugal; the arms were adopted on 29 June 1892. The main feature is an eagle holding in its talons branches of sugar cane and olive.

RIO GRANDE DO NORTE

Flag adopted 3 December 1957.
Proportions 2:3.

The colours of the flag represent the forests and the chalk cliffs. The arms were adopted on 1 July 1909.

RIO GRANDE DO SUL

STATE FLAG

Flag introduced in 1891.
Proportions 7:10.

This design was adopted by the republic of Rio Grande do Sul in 1836. The arms, displaying a Phrygian cap of liberty and suits of armour, were added in 1891.

State flags on Brazilian postage stamps (*from left to right beginning top right*) Ceará; Espirito Santo; Paraíba; Rio Grande do Norte; Rondônia.

An almost identical flag with 21 stripes, designed in 1888, was one of several proposed flags for the Republic of Brazil. It did not become the national flag but was used unofficially as the flag of the state of São Paulo. The number of stripes was reduced in 1932. The white, black and red represent whites, blacks and Native Americans living peacefully together. Blue and white are the historic colours of Portugal, and blue, white and red are the republican colours.

SERGIPE
Flag introduced 1897. Proportions 7:10.

The colours of the flag are those of the national flag of Brazil. The stars are those of the Southern Cross constellation.

TOCANTINS

STATE FLAG

Flag adopted 1 January 1989. Proportions 3:5.

The sun represents the state, which split from Goías in 1988. The blue symbolizes river Tocantins.

URUGUAY

Oriental Republic of Uruguay, Spanish **República Oriental del Uruguay**. Republic in SE South America.

NATIONAL FLAG AND ENSIGN

Adopted 12 July 1830. Proportions 2:3.

RONDÔNIA
Flag adopted 31 December 1981. Proportions 7:10.

The flag shows the colours of the Brazilian flag, yellow and green. The star stands for the state.

RORAIMA

STATE FLAG

Flag adopted 31 December 1981. Proportions 7:10.

The flag displays the colours of the national flag of Brazil, yellow and green. The star represents the state and the red line symbolizes the Equator.

SANTA CATARINA
Flag adopted 23 October 1953. Proportions 3:4.

The green lozenge represents the vegetation of the state; the arms were adopted on 15 August 1895. The star symbolizes the state and the Phrygian cap is a symbol of liberty. The eagle represents productivity, the anchor denotes the maritime character of the state and the key indicates that it is the key to southern Brazil. The wreath, made of grain and coffee plants, symbolizes agriculture.

SÃO PAULO

STATE FLAG

Flag adopted 18 November 1932. Proportions 7:10.

The creators of the flag were inspired by the national colours of Argentina, and by the design of the American Stars and Stripes. It was adopted on 16 December 1828, with nine blue and ten white stripes. In 1830 the number of stripes was reduced to four blue and five white; these nine stripes represent the nine original regions of Uruguay. The sun is a symbol of freedom.

PARAGUAY

Republic of Paraguay,
Spanish **República del Paraguay**.
Republic in S Central South America.

NATIONAL FLAG AND ENSIGN, OBVERSE

EMBLEM IN THE CENTRE OF THE REVERSE OF
THE NATIONAL FLAG AND ENSIGN

Adopted 25 November 1842. Proportions 1:2.

This is the only national flag in the world with a different design on the obverse and reverse. The state seal appears on the obverse and the reverse is charged with the treasury seal. Red, white and blue are the republican colours. They symbolize patriotism, courage, equality and justice (red), steadfastness, unity, peace and the purity of ideas (white), kindliness, love, sharpness, sense of reality, and liberty (blue). The star symbolizes the date of independence, 14 May 1811. The lion guarding the Phrygian cap symbolizes the defence of liberty. The national motto is "Peace and Justice".

BOLIVIA

Republic of Bolivia,
Spanish **República de Bolivia**.
Republic in W Central South America.

STATE FLAG

*Adopted 5 November 1851. Proportions 2:3.
Civil flag and ensign are without arms.*

The red symbolizes the blood of the national heroes, sacrifice and love. The yellow stands for the mineral resources and for the Incas, who were the first to make use of them. The green is a symbol of eternal hope, evolution and progress.

The arms display symbols of dignity and independence (condor), liberty (sun) and republic (Phrygian cap). The animal kingdom is represented by an alpaca, the mineral kingdom by Mount Potosi and the vegetable kingdom by a breadfruit tree. The wheatsheaf symbolizes agriculture. The ten stars represent the nine departments of Bolivia and the one lost to Chile. The flags and weapons symbolize the will to defend the country.

PERU

Republic of Peru,
Spanish **República del Perú**.
Republic in W South America.

STATE FLAG AND ENSIGN

*Adopted 25 February 1825. Proportions 2:3.
The civil flag and ensign do not have arms.*

According to legend, General José de San Martin saw a great number of flamingos when he arrived in Peru in 1820. Taking this as a good omen, he decided that white and red should be the colours of the Peruvian Legion that he founded to liberate Peru. The white represents peace, dignity and progress; the red symbolizes war and courage. The arms show symbols of the animal kingdom (*vicuña*), vegetable kingdom (cinchona tree) and mineral kingdom (a cornucopia full of gold and silver coins). The laurel wreath above the shield symbolizes the republic. The palm and laurel wreath around the shield is a symbol of peace and the will to defend the country.

CHILE

Republic of Chile,
Spanish **República de Chile**.
Republic in SW South America.

NATIONAL FLAG AND ENSIGN

Adopted 18 October 1817. Proportions 2:3.

The flag was designed by an American, Charles Wood, who fought for Chilean independence as an officer in the army of General José de San Martin. The design is clearly influenced by the Stars and Stripes. The white star is the guiding star on the path of progress and honour. The blue symbolizes the sky; the white symbolizes the snow of the Andes, and the red stands for all the blood shed in the struggle for independence.

ARGENTINA

Republic of Argentina,
Spanish **República Argentina**.
Republic in S South America.

NATIONAL FLAG AND ENSIGN

Adopted 25 February 1818.
Proportions unspecified.

In May 1810 the pro-independence movement initiated the use of the blue and white cockade. It was decreed the national cockade on 18 February 1812, and nine days later a flag in these colours was adopted. The blue and white symbolize the clear skies and snow of the Andes. The sun, added in 1818, is the *Sol de Mayo* ("May Sun"), the national symbol of Argentina. It commemorates the appearance of the sun in cloudy skies on 25 May 1810, when the first mass demonstration in favour of independence took place.

The flag with the sun was the state flag and the state and war ensign. Since 16 August 1985 it may also be used as the civil flag and ensign.

THE SOUTH ATLANTIC

FALKLAND ISLANDS

British crown colony in the S Atlantic.

STATE FLAG AND ENSIGN

Introduced in 1948. Proportions 1:2.

The badge in the centre of the fly portion of the British blue ensign contains the arms, granted on 29 September 1948. The ram, standing on tussock grass, denotes that wool is the principal product of the islands. The ship is *Desire* which was commanded by Captain John Davis in 1592 when he discovered the Falklands. The five stars on its sail allude to the Southern Cross constellation.

SOUTH GEORGIA AND SOUTH SANDWICH ISLANDS

British crown colony in the S Atlantic.

STATE FLAG AND ENSIGN

Introduced in 1992. Proportions 1:2.

The British blue ensign is charged with the shield of arms, granted on 14 February 1992. The colours white, blue and green represent ice, snow and grass respectively. The lion is a symbol of British protection and the torch symbolizes exploration. The stars are from the arms of Captain James Cook, who discovered the islands in 1775.

BRITISH ANTARCTIC TERRITORY

British dependent territory in the S Atlantic.

FLAG AND ENSIGN OF THE RESEARCH STATIONS
AND THEIR VESSELS

Adopted 21 April 1998. Proportions 1:2.

This ensign is flown by Natural Environment Research Council vessels engaged on British Antarctic survey work. The ensign features the only use of a white field with the Union Jack in the canton. The arms were granted to the Falkland Islands' Dependencies on 11 March 1952 and with the crest added in 1963 they were assigned to the new colony. The torch is a symbol of exploration; the white field with wavy blue stripes is the ice-covered land and the Antarctic waters. The shield is supported by the British lion and a penguin which represents the local fauna. The crest shows the research ship "Discovery".

SAINT HELENA

British-crown colony in the SE Atlantic.

STATE FLAG AND ENSIGN

Introduced in 1984. Proportions 1:2.

The British blue ensign is charged with the shield of arms, granted on 30 January 1984. The ship recalls that in 1659 the island became the possession of the British East India Company. The wirebird is endemic to the island.

Flags of Africa

The current national flags of the countries of Africa, from Morocco and Algeria to Anjouan and Mauritius, and their territories, states and provinces are illustrated and described in the following pages.

For ease of reference, the countries of this continent have been divided into geographical areas. We begin in northern Africa and move on through western, central and eastern Africa. Finally we look at the flags of the countries of southern Africa and the islands of the Indian Ocean.

For each entry, the country or territory's name is given in its most easily recognized form and then in all its official languages. This is followed by a description of its political status and geographic position. The basic data for each flag contains the status of the flag, date of adoption, proportions, and symbolic meaning.

NORTH AFRICA

MOROCCO

Kingdom of Morocco,
Arabic **al-Mamlaka al-Maghrebia**.
Constitutional monarchy in NW Africa.

NATIONAL FLAG, CIVIL AND STATE ENSIGN

Adopted 17 November 1915. Proportions 2:3.

The red is the colour of the sheriffs of Mecca. The pentagram, called the "Seal of Solomon", is an ancient symbol of life and good health.

ALGERIA

Democratic and Popular Republic of Algeria, Arabic **al-Jumhuriya al-Jazariya ad-Dimuqratiya ash-Shabiya**.
Republic in N Africa.

NATIONAL FLAG AND ENSIGN

Adopted 3 July 1962. Proportions 2:3.

The colours of the flag symbolize Islam (green), purity (white) and liberty (red). The crescent and star is a symbol of Islam, with the crescent being more closed than in other Muslim countries because the Algerians believe that the long horns of the crescent bring happiness.

TUNISIA

Tunisian Republic,
Arabic **al-Jumhuriya at-Tunisiya**.
Republic in N Africa.

NATIONAL FLAG AND ENSIGN

Introduced c.1835. Proportions 2:3.

The flag is based on that of Turkey. Until 1850 the star had six points. The star and crescent stand for Islam.

LIBYA

Great Socialist People's Libyan Arab Republic, Arabic **al-Jamahariya al-Arabiya al-Libya al-shabiya al-Ishtirakiya al-Uzma**.
Socialist republic in N Central Africa.

NATIONAL FLAG AND ENSIGN

Introduced in 1977. Proportions 1:2.

This is the only monochromatic national flag in the world. The green is the colour of Islam and is a manifestation of the Green Revolution proclaimed by President Mu'ammar al Qaddafi.

EGYPT

Arab Republic of Egypt,
Arabic **Jumhuriyat Misr al-Arabiya**.
Republic in NE Africa.

CIVIL AND STATE FLAG AND ENSIGN

Officially hoisted 5 October 1984.
Proportions 2:3.

The red-white-black horizontal tricolour was introduced in Egypt after the revolution of 1953. The central white stripe was charged with two green stars from 1958 to 1972, and with the hawk of Quraish from 1972 to 1984. In 1984 it was replaced by the eagle of Saladin, standing on a panel that carries the name of the country. The eagle bears on its breast a shield, sometimes in the national colours.

SOME HISTORIC FLAGS

While formally part of the Ottoman Empire, in the 18th and 19th centuries Algeria, Tunisia and Tripoli (Libya) each had their own civil ensigns. All the ensigns displayed between five and seven horizontal stripes: white-red-green (Algeria), blue-red-green (Tunisia) and red-green-white (Tripoli). While under foreign domination, Algeria (which was under French rule from 1830-1962) and Libya (under Italian rule from 1912-1947) did not have their own flags. After achieving independence, however, they have made changes to their national flags several times.

WESTERN AFRICA

WESTERN SAHARA

Sahara Arab Democratic Republic, Arabic **al-Jumhuriya as-Sahrawiya ad-Dimukratiya al-Arabiya**.

State in W Africa currently occupied by Morocco.

NATIONAL FLAG

Introduced 27 February 1976. Proportions 1:2.

Western Sahara proclaimed independence and adopted its flag the day after the formal Spanish withdrawal. The design of the flag is based on that of Palestine, with pan-Arab colours and a red crescent and star, the symbol of Islam. The red symbolizes blood shed in the struggle for independence, the black recalls the period of colonialism, the white stands for liberty and the green is a symbol of progress.

MAURITANIA

Islamic Republic of Mauritania, French **République Islamique Arabe et Africaine de Mauritanie**, Arabic **al-Jumhuriya al-Islamiya al-Mauritaniya**.

Islamic republic in W Africa.

NATIONAL FLAG AND ENSIGN

Adopted 1 April 1959. Proportions 2:3.

The green and the crescent and star are both symbols of Islam; the green also represents hope for a bright future. The yellow stands for the Sahara Desert.

MALI

Republic of Mali, French **République du Mali**.

Republic in W Africa.

NATIONAL FLAG AND ENSIGN

Adopted 1 March 1961. Proportions 2:3.

The flag, based on the French *Tricolore*, displays the pan-African colours. They stand for nature (green), purity and mineral resources (yellow), and for bravery and blood shed in the struggle for independence (red).

SENEGAL

Republic of Senegal, French **République du Sénégal**.

Republic in W Africa.

NATIONAL FLAG AND ENSIGN

Introduced in 1960. Proportions 2:3.

After the dissolution of the federation with Mali, Senegal retained the colours of the flag and placed a green star in the centre, symbolizing unity and hope. The green is an expression of hope for undisturbed progress, the yellow represents the verdant land and the wealth which will be the fruit of collective labour. The red recalls the martyrs and the common struggle of the African nations for independence; it is also a symbol of life and socialism.

THE GAMBIA

Republic of the Gambia.

Republic in W Africa.

NATIONAL FLAG, CIVIL AND STATE ENSIGN

Introduced 18 February 1965. Proportions 2:3.

The original idea for the flag came from the Gambia, but the design was prepared by the College of Arms in London. The red stands for the sun, the blue represents the river Gambia and the green symbolizes the fertile land and agriculture. The white stripes stand for unity and peace.

GUINEA-BISSAU

Republic of Guinea-Bissau, Portuguese **República da Guiné-Bissau**.

Republic in W Africa.

NATIONAL FLAG AND ENSIGN

Introduced 24 September 1973. Proportions 1:2.

In August 1961 the African Party for the Independence of Guinea and Cape Verde adopted a flag in pan-African colours with the party initials (PAIGC) beneath a black star. When independence was proclaimed the flag, without the initials, became the national flag of Guinea-Bissau.

The red stands for the suffering under colonial rule and for the blood shed in the struggle for independence. The yellow symbolizes the fruits of work that contribute to well-being. The green represents the tropical forests of the country and hope for a bright future. The star is a symbol of Africa and its people.

GUINEA

Republic of Guinea,
French **République de Guinée**.
Republic in W Africa.

NATIONAL FLAG AND ENSIGN

Adopted 10 November 1958. Proportions 2:3.

The first French colony to achieve independence, Guinea patterned its flag on the French *Tricolore*. Sékou Touré, the first President of Guinea, stated that by choosing the same colours as those of Ghana his country intended to show its dedication to African unity. The colours reflect the national motto "Work, Justice, Solidarity". The red is the colour of blood and reflects the spirit of sacrifice and hard work, and symbolizes the will for progress. The yellow is the colour of the gold of Guinea and of the African sun, which is the source of energy, generosity and equality as it shines on everyone. The green is the colour of the vegetation, agriculture, the productivity of the peasants and the spirit of solidarity in collective enterprises. Thus the three colours of the flag symbolize the three bases of the republic: labour, justice and solidarity.

SIERRA LEONE

Republic of Sierra Leone.
Republic in W Africa.

NATIONAL FLAG

Officially hoisted 27 April 1961. Proportions 2:3.

The green represents the agriculture, natural resources and the mountains. The white stands for unity and justice. The blue is a symbol of hope that the only natural harbour in Freetown will be able to make its contribution to peace throughout the world.

LIBERIA

Republic of Liberia.Republic in W Africa.

NATIONAL FLAG

Adopted 27 August 1847. Proportions 10:19.

The design of the flag copies that of the United States, from where since 1822 freed slaves came to settle in Liberia. The white star represents the shining light of the new republic in the dark continent, represented by a blue square. The 11 stripes symbolize the 11 signatories of the Liberian Declaration of Independence.

IVORY COAST

Republic of Côte d'Ivoire, French **République de la Côte d'Ivoire**.
Republic in W Africa.

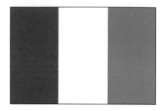

NATIONAL FLAG AND ENSIGN

Adopted 3 December 1959. Proportions 2:3.

The flag is based on the French *Tricolore*. The orange represents the savannahs of the north and the spirit of national development. The green stands for the forests in the south and for the hope of a better future based on natural resources. The white is the colour of the sky and purity, symbolizing unity between the north and south of the country.

BURKINA FASO

The People's Democratic Republic of Burkina Faso, French **République Démocratique Populaire de Burkina Faso**.
Socialist republic in W Africa.

NATIONAL FLAG

Adopted 4 August 1984. Proportions 2:3.

The red is a symbol of revolutionary concern to transform the country and the green symbolizes hope and abundance. The star stands for the revolution, leading the nation to a golden future. The yellow represents the undiscovered mineral resources.

GHANA

Republic of Ghana. Republic in W Africa.

NATIONAL FLAG AND STATE ENSIGN

Adopted 6 March 1957. Proportions 2:3.

Ghana was the first country in black Africa to use the Ethiopian colours, which have since been called pan-African. The black star symbolizes the lodestar of African freedom. The red commemorates those who worked for independence, the gold (yellow) represents the wealth of the country (its former name was the Gold Coast) and the green stands for forests and farms.

TOGO

Republic of Togo,
French **République Togolaise**.
Republic in W Africa.

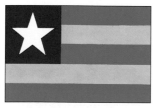

NATIONAL FLAG AND ENSIGN

Adopted 27 April 1960. Proportions 2:3.

The green symbolizes hope and the yellow signifies faith in work as the way to achieve material, moral and spiritual well-being. The red is a symbol of charity, fidelity and love, the virtues that make people love their neighbours and sacrifice their own lives, if necessary, for the triumph of the principles of humanity and the lessening

of human misery. The white is the colour of purity, reminding all citizens to be worthy of their nation's independence.

BENIN

People's Republic of Benin, French
République Populaire du Benin.
Socialist republic in W Africa.

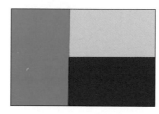

NATIONAL FLAG AND ENSIGN

*Adopted 16 November 1959, re-established
1 August 1990. Proportions 2:3.*

The green denotes hope for renewal, the red evokes the ancestors' courage and the yellow refers to the country's riches.

CAPE VERDE

Republic of Cape Verde, Portuguese
República de Cabo Verde.
Republic comprising an archipelago
in the Atlantic, W Africa.

NATIONAL FLAG AND ENSIGN

*Officially hoisted 25 September 1992.
Proportions 10:17.*

The ring of stars symbolizes the unity of all parts of the country. The ten stars represent the ten main islands of the archipelago: São Tiago, Santo Antão, São Vincente, São Nicolau, Sal, Boa Vista, Fogo, Maio, Brava and Santa Luzia. The colours symbolize the

sky and the sea (blue), peace (white) and the efforts of the people (red).

NIGERIA

Federal Republic of Nigeria.
Federal republic in W Africa.

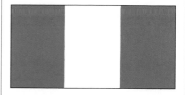

NATIONAL FLAG

Officially hoisted 1 October 1960. Proportions 1:2.

The green reflects the green land of Nigeria and stands for its agriculture. The white symbolizes peace.

SÃO TOMÉ AND PRÍNCIPE

**Democratic Republic of São Tomé and
Príncipe**, Portuguese **República Democrática
de São Tomé and Príncipe**.
Republic consisting of several islands
in the Gulf of Guinea.

NATIONAL FLAG AND ENSIGN

Adopted 5 November 1975. Proportions 1:2.

The two stars represent the two main islands of the nation: São Tomé and Príncipe. The red stands for the blood shed in the struggle for independence, the green is the colour of the rich vegetation and the yellow represents cocoa, which is one of the main agricultural products.

CENTRAL AFRICA

NIGER

Republic of Niger,
French **République du Niger**.
Republic in N Central Africa.

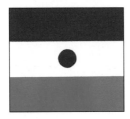

NATIONAL FLAG

Adopted 23 November 1959.
Proportions unspecified.

The orange represents the Sahara Desert, with the white being a symbol of purity and innocence. The orange disc represents the sun and symbolizes the sacrifices made by the people, their firm commitment and their determination to defend human rights and justice. The green, a symbol of hope, represents the fertile and productive zone of Niger.

CHAD

Republic of Chad,
French **République du Tchad**.
Republic in N Central Africa.

NATIONAL FLAG

Adopted 6 November 1959. Proportions 2:3.

The blue represents the rivers and forests, the yellow symbolizes sand and the desert, and the red is a symbol of sacrifice and the blood of martyrs.

CAMEROON

Republic of Cameroon,
French **République du Cameroun**.
Republic in W Central Africa.

NATIONAL FLAG AND ENSIGN

Adopted 20 May 1975. Proportions 2:3.

The green stands for the luxuriant vegetation of the south, and also represents hope for a rich, prosperous, hard-working and unified Cameroon. The red is a symbol of sovereignty and of unity between the north and the south. The yellow represents the soil of the north, wealth and the sun. The star symbolizes unity.

CENTRAL AFRICAN REPUBLIC

French **République Centrafricaine**.
Republic in W Central Africa.

NATIONAL FLAG

Introduced 1 December 1958.
Proportions unspecified.

The flag displays the colours of France (blue-white-red) combined with the pan-African colours (green-yellow-red) to show that Europeans and Africans should have respect and friendship for one another. Their common bond, their red blood, is represented by the vertical red stripe binding all the stripes together. The star symbolizes independence.

EQUATORIAL GUINEA

Republic of Equatorial Guinea,
Spanish **República de Guinea Ecuatorial**.
Republic in W Central Africa.

NATIONAL FLAG AND ENSIGN

Adopted 12 October 1968, re-adopted
21 August 1979. Proportions unspecified.

The blue represents the sea linking the mainland of the country with Bioko and other islands. The colour green symbolizes its tropical forests and natural riches, the white stands for peace and the red commemorates the blood shed in the struggle for independence. The main device of the arms is the tree under which King Bonkoro signed the treaty with Spain in 1843. The six stars represent the six districts of the state.

GABON

Gabonese Republic,
French **République Gabonaise**.
Republic in W Central Africa.

NATIONAL FLAG AND ENSIGN

Adopted 9 August 1960. Proportions 3:4.

The design of the flag was inspired by the geographical position of Gabon. The green (forests) and the blue (Atlantic Ocean) are separated by the yellow stripe, which stands for the Equator and the ever-present sun.

CONGO

Republic of Congo, French **République du Congo**. Republic in Central Africa.

NATIONAL FLAG

Adopted 18 August 1959, re-established 10 June 1991. Proportions 2:3.

The green stands for nature and peace. The yellow represents the natural wealth and expresses hope for a better future. The red is a symbol of independence and of the dignity of all humanity.

CONGO

Democratic Republic of Congo, French **République Démocratique du Congo**. Republic in Central Africa.

NATIONAL FLAG AND ENSIGN

Adopted 30 June 1960, re-adopted 17 May 1997. Proportions 2:3.

The blue flag with a large yellow star in the centre was the flag of Congo from 1885 to 1960, when the six stars along the hoist were

added. The blue symbolizes the river Congo and the star symbolizes a bright future. The six stars represent the six provinces existing at the time of independence.

RWANDA

Republic of Rwanda, Kinyarwanda **Republika yha Rwanda**, French **République Rwandaise**. Republic in E Central Africa.

NATIONAL FLAG

Adopted 28 January 1961. Proportions 2:3.

The red represents the blood and pain suffered in the struggle for independence, the yellow is a symbol of tranquillity and peace, and the green represents hope and

EASTERN AFRICA

SUDAN

Democratic Republic of Sudan, Arabic **Jumhuriyat es-Sudan**. Military republic in NE Africa.

NATIONAL FLAG AND ENSIGN

Officially hoisted 20 May 1970. Proportions 1:2.

The red stands for struggles and for the martyrs in the Sudan and the great Arab land. The white is the colour of peace, optimism, light and love. The black

optimism. The initial "R" for Rwanda has been added to differentiate the flag from that of Guinea.

BURUNDI

Republic of Burundi, Kirundi **Republika y'Uburundi**, French **République du Burundi**. Republic in E Central Africa.

STATE FLAG

Adopted 26 December 1968. Proportions 3:5 (established 27 September 1982).

The colours represent the struggle for independence (red), hope (green) and peace (white). The three stars symbolize the national motto "Unity, Work, Progress".

represents the Sudan and the Mahdija Revolution, during which a black flag was used. The green symbolizes Islamic prosperity and agriculture.

ERITREA

State of Eritrea, Tigrinya **Hagere Eritrea**. Republic in NE Africa.

NATIONAL FLAG

Adopted 24 May 1993. Proportions 1:2.

The basic design of the flag is identical to the flag of the Eritrean People's Liberation Front. The olive wreath with an upright branch in the centre recalls the emblem on the first flag of Eritrea (1952).

ETHIOPIA

Federal Democratic Republic of Ethiopia,
Amharic **Hebretesebawit Ityopia**.
Republic in NE Africa.

STATE FLAG

Adopted 6 February 1996. Proportions 1:2.

The Ethiopian horizontal tricolour dates back to *c.*1895. In 1996 the new national emblem was placed in the centre of the flag. The blue symbolizes peace and the pentagram represents the unity of the nations, nationalities and peoples of Ethiopia.

The original symbolism of the colours denoted the Christian virtues. In the present official symbolism, the green represents fertility, labour and development; the yellow, hope, justice and equality; and the red, sacrifice and heroism in the cause of freedom and equality.

DJIBOUTI

Republic of Djibouti, French **République de Djibouti**, Arabic **Jumhuriya Djibouti**.
Republic in NE Africa.

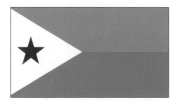

NATIONAL FLAG AND ENSIGN

Officially hoisted 27 June 1977.
Proportions 21:38.

The colours of the flag stand for the sea and sky (blue), the earth (green) and peace (white). Green and blue are also the colours of the two main population groups, the Afars and Issas respectively. The red star recalls the struggle for independence and is a symbol of unity.

SOMALILAND

Republic of Somaliland, Somali **Jamhuriyadda Somaliland**.
De facto independent republic in NE Africa.

NATIONAL FLAG AND ENSIGN

Introduced 14 October 1996.
Proportions unspecified.

The flag displays the pan-Arab colours; the star stands for the republic. On the green stripe is *Shahada*, the Muslim Statement of Faith.

SOMALIA

Somali Democratic Republic, Somali **Jamhuriyadda Dimugradiga ee Soomaliya**.
Republic in E Africa.

NATIONAL FLAG AND ENSIGN

Officially introduced 12 October 1954.
Proportions unspecified.

The adoption of the blue was influenced by the blue field of the United Nations flag. The five points of the star represent the five countries in which the Somalis live: Somali (Italian colony), British Somali, Ethiopia, Kenya and Djibouti.

KENYA

Republic of Kenya,
Kiswahili **Jamhuri ya Kenya**.
Republic in E Africa.

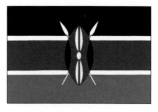

NATIONAL FLAG, CIVIL AND STATE ENSIGN

Officially introduced 12 December 1963.
Proportions 2:3.

The colours symbolize the people (black), the struggle for independence (red) and agriculture (green). The white stripes stand for peace and unity. The Masai shield and spears represent the will to defend freedom.

UGANDA

Republic of Uganda,
Kiswahili **Jamhuri ya Uganda**.
Republic in E Central Africa.

NATIONAL FLAG

Officially hoisted 9 October 1962.
Proportions unspecified.

The colours of the flag derive from the flag of the Uganda People's Congress, the party that won the first elections. They symbolize the people of Africa (black), sunshine (yellow) and brotherhood (red). The crested crane (*Balearica pavonia*) is the symbol of Uganda and has already appeared on the colonial badge in the early 20th century.

TANZANIA

United Republic of Tanzania, Kiswahili **Jamhuri ya Muungano wa Tanzania**.
Republic in E Africa.

NATIONAL FLAG AND ENSIGN

Adopted 30 June 1964. Proportions 2:3.

The colours of the flag combine those of the flags of Tanganyika (green, yellow, black) and Zanzibar (blue, black, green). They symbolize the people (black), the land (green), the sea (blue) and the mineral wealth (yellow).

TANZANIA

The red flag of the Sultanate of Zanzibar dated from the 18th century. On 12 January 1964 the sultan was overthrown and the new republic adopted a flag with three vertical stripes of blue, yellow, and green. Less than three weeks later the flag was changed to a horizontal tricolour of blue, black and green. At that time, Tanganyika's flag was green with a black horizontal stripe fimbriated yellow and positioned in the centre of the flag. In April 1964 the two formed a united republic, combining the two flags into the flag that we see today.

MOZAMBIQUE

People's Republic of Mozambique, Portuguese **República Popular de Moçambique**.
Republic in SE Africa.

NATIONAL FLAG AND ENSIGN

Introduced in April 1983.
Proportions unspecified.

The flag follows the design of the Frelimo Party flag. The star symbolizes the spirit of international solidarity. The book, hoe and gun stand for study, production and defence. The red recalls "the centuries of resistance to colonialism, the armed national liberation struggle, and the defence of sovereignty". The other colours represent the riches of the soil (green), the African continent (black), the mineral riches (yellow), and justice and peace (white).

MALAWI

Republic of Malawi, Chichewa **Mfuko la Malawi**.
Republic in SE Africa.

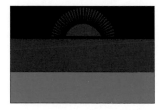

NATIONAL FLAG

Officially hoisted 6 July 1964. Proportions 2:3.

The leading force in the struggle for independence was the Malawi Congress Party. Its flag, a horizontal tricolour of

black-red-green, served as the basis for the national flag. A sun emblem was added to symbolize the dawn of hope and freedom for the whole of Africa. The black stands for the people of Africa, the red symbolizes the blood of the martyrs of African freedom, and the green represents the vegetation of Malawi.

ZAMBIA

Republic of Zambia.
Republic in S Central Africa.

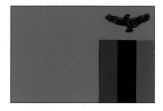

NATIONAL FLAG

Officially hoisted 24 October 1964. Shape of the eagle modified in 1996. Proportions 2:3.

The eagle in flight symbolizes freedom in Zambia and the ability to rise above the country's problems. The red represents the struggle for independence, the black the people of Zambia, the orange its mineral wealth and the green its natural resources.

ANGOLA

Republic of Angola, Portuguese **República de Angola**.
Republic in SW Africa.

NATIONAL FLAG AND ENSIGN

Introduced 11 November 1975. Proportions 2:3.

The red symbolizes the blood shed in the struggle for independence. The black stands for Africa. The cog-wheel and machete are symbols of the workers and peasants respectively. The star symbolizes international solidarity and progress. The yellow signifies the wealth of the nation.

NAMIBIA

Republic of Namibia.
Republic in SW Africa.

NATIONAL FLAG AND ENSIGN

Adopted 21 March 1990. Proportions 2:3.

The sun symbolizes life and energy. The golden yellow represents the plains and the Namib Desert. The blue represents the sky, the Atlantic Ocean, the marine resources of Namibia, and the importance of rain and water. The red stands for the people, their heroism and their determination to build a future of equal opportunity for all. The green is a symbol of the vegetation and natural resources. The white refers to peace and unity.

BOTSWANA

Republic of Botswana.
Republic in S Central Africa.

NATIONAL FLAG

Officially hoisted 30 September 1966. Proportions 2:3.

The blue symbolizes the sky and reliance on water. The black and white represent the majority and minority of the country's population respectively.

ZIMBABWE

Republic of Zimbabwe.
Republic in S Central Africa.

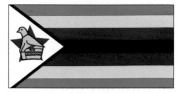

NATIONAL FLAG AND ENSIGN

Officially introduced 18 April 1980. Proportions 1:2.

The emblem displays a red star, representing socialism, and the Great Zimbabwe Bird, which represents the great past of the country. The colours of the flag symbolize the majority of the population (black), the blood shed in the struggle for independence (red), the mineral wealth (yellow), the agriculture (green) and peace (white).

SOUTH AFRICA

Republic of South Africa,
Afrikaans **Republiek van Suid-Afrika**.
Republic in S Africa.

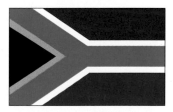

NATIONAL FLAG, CIVIL AND STATE ENSIGN

Officially introduced 27 April 1994. Proportions 2:3.

The flag combines the colours of the Boer republics (red, white, blue) with the colours of the African National Congress (black,

green, yellow), which came to power in 1994. The ANC is shown as a driving force behind the country's convergence and unification which is symbolized by the "Y" shape.

LESOTHO

Kingdom of Lesotho,
Lesotho **Mmuso wa Lesotho**.
Constitutional monarchy in S Africa.

NATIONAL FLAG

Officially introduced 20 January 1987. Proportions 2:3.

The colours of the flag symbolize peace (white), rain (blue) and prosperity (green). The Lesotho shield with weapons symbolizes a will to defend the country.

SWAZILAND

Kingdom of Swaziland,
Swazi **Umbuso we Swatini**.
Absolute monarchy in SE Africa.

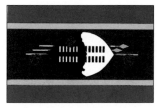

STATE FLAG

Adopted 30 October 1967. Proportions 2:3.

The red symbolizes the battles of the past, the yellow represents the wealth of the country's resources and the blue stands for peace. The black and white Swazi shield is that of the Emasotha Regiment, formed in the late 1920s. Behind the shield appear their assegais and a traditional fighting stick with *tinjobo* tassels, made from widow-bird and loury feathers.

MADAGASCAR

Democratic Republic of Madagascar, Malagasy **Repoblika Demokratika n`i Madagaskar**.
Republic comprising an island in the Indian Ocean.

NATIONAL FLAG AND ENSIGN

Adopted in October 1958. Proportions 2:3.

The choice of colours for the national flag was influenced by the fact that white and red were the flags of the Hova Empire in the 19th century. The green was added for the peoples living on the coast. The colours symbolize purity (white), sovereignty (red) and hope (green).

COMOROS

Federal Islamic Republic of Comoros, Arabic **Jumhuriyat al-Qumur al-Ittihadiya al-Islamiya**, Comorian **Dja Mouhouri Yamtsangagniho ya Kissilam ya Komori**.
Republic consisting of Grand Comore island in the Indian Ocean.

NATIONAL FLAG AND ENSIGN

Adopted 3 October 1996. Proportions 2:3.

The green field and the crescent stand for Islam. The four stars represent the four islands of the archipelago, despite the fact that Mayotte, Anjouan and Mohéli are separate political entities. The word "Allah" appears in the upper fly corner, and the word "Muhammad" in the lower hoist.

ANJOUAN

State of Anjouan
De facto independent country comprising an island in the Indian Ocean.

NATIONAL FLAG AND ENSIGN

Approved on 25 February 1998. Proportions 2:3.

The red flag with a right hand and a crescent was used by the Sultanate of Anjouan in the 19th century. Red was for centuries the colour of the Arab colonies along the coast of eastern Africa and on the islands in the Indian Ocean, and the crescent is the symbol of Islam.

SEYCHELLES

Republic of Seychelles, Creole **Repibik Sesel**.
Republic consisting of a group of islands in the Indian Ocean.

NATIONAL FLAG AND ENSIGN

Adopted 8 January 1996. Proportions 1:2.

The flag is a combination of the colours of the two main political parties, the Democratic Party (which is represented by blue and yellow) and the Seychelles People's United Party (represented by red, white and green). The blue symbolizes the sky and the sea; the yellow represents the sun; red stands for the people and their determination to work in unity; white symbolizes social justice and harmony; and green stands for the land.

MAURITIUS

Republic of Mauritius.
Republic comprising an island in the Indian Ocean.

NATIONAL FLAG

Officially hoisted 12 March 1968. Proportions 2:3.

The red stripe represents the struggle for freedom and independence, the blue stripe stands for the colour of the Indian Ocean. The yellow stripe symbolizes the new light of independence, and the green stripe represents agriculture and symbolizes the colour of lush, green Mauritius throughout the year.

Flags of International Organizations

These flags are presented in chronological order, beginning with the flag of the Red Cross, which has existed since 1863. The latest addition to the family of international organizations is the Portuguese-speaking community, whose flag was adopted in 1996.

THE RED CROSS

The International Committee of the Red Cross was established in 1863. Its activities follow the Geneva Conventions of 1864, 1907, 1929, 1947 and 1977 on the treatment of prisoners of war and the protection of civilians during hostilities and natural catastrophes.

The flag was proposed by the Red Cross's founder, the Swiss philanthropist Henri Dunant, and was adopted in 1863 as the flag of Switzerland in reversed colours. The flag used in Muslim countries, which was adopted in 1876, displays a red Muslim crescent instead of the cross.

THE COMMONWEALTH

Originally the members of the Common-wealth of Nations were the United Kingdom and its self-governing Dominions. The term "British Commonwealth" began to be used after World War I. In 1949 the name was changed to the Commonwealth and in 1965 the Commonwealth Secretariat in London was established. A total of 54 independent countries from all parts of the world belong to the Commonwealth.

The flag displays the letter "C" (as the first letter of "Commonwealth") which encircles a central globe, denoting the global scope of the organization. The number of lines forming the letter "C" does not correspond to the number of member-states.

LEAGUE OF ARAB STATES

The main aim of the Arab League is to protect the independence and sovereignty of the 22 member-states, and to safeguard their interests. The flag was adopted in 1945, the year the organization was founded. The green and the crescent symbolize Islam and the name of the organization appears in the centre of the emblem. The chain is a symbol of unity and the laurel wreath stands for peace as well as dignity.

UNITED NATIONS

The United Nations was established in 1945 to promote international peace, security and co-operation. It is the largest and the most important international organization, with 185 member-states. Its specialized departments handle international issues including economic, monetary, scientific, educational, social, judicial and health matters.

The flag was adopted on 20 October 1947. The colour blue and the olive branches symbolize peace, and the map of the world represents the organization's global concerns.

SOUTH PACIFIC COMMISSION

The South Pacific Commission was set up in 1947 to advise the governments of Australia, New Zealand, Great Britain, France, the Netherlands and the United States on economic, social and health matters affecting the territories in the South Pacific administered by them. At present the Commission has 27 member-states. The emblem, formed by the letter "C" and a ring of stars, resembles an atoll. The six points of the stars symbolize the original six members of the Commission and the number of stars represents the number of member-states.

ORGANIZATION OF AMERICAN STATES

This name and the charter of the organization were adopted in 1948. The main goal of the member-states of OAS is to uphold sovereignty and to work for peace and prosperity in the region. The flag, adopted in 1965, has been modified several times as the flags of new member-states were added to the emblem; currently the emblem displays the flags of 35 member-states.

NORTH ATLANTIC TREATY ORGANIZATION

NATO was formed in 1949 by the countries of western Europe and North America, originally as a united defence against the threat of Soviet aggression. The flag was adopted in 1954. Its dark blue field represents the Atlantic Ocean, the circle is a symbol of unity and the compass symbolizes the common direction towards peace that has been taken by the 19 member-nations.

ORGANIZATION OF PETROLEUM EXPORTING COUNTRIES

OPEC was set up in 1961 by the main oil-producing countries and currently has 11 members; the flag was adopted in 1970. The emblem is formed from the stylized letters "OPEC".

ORGANIZATION OF AFRICAN UNITY

The OAU was formed in 1963 and includes all independent African countries. Its aim is mutual co-operation and peaceful settlement of conflicts. The colours of the flag, adopted in 1970, symbolize the natural environment of Africa (green), its golden future (golden yellow) and a peaceful co-existence (white). The emblem is a golden map of Africa encircled by a golden wreath.

ASSOCIATION OF SOUTH-EAST ASIAN NATIONS

ASEAN was formed in 1967 to promote regional stability and economic co-operation. The flag, adopted in 1997, displays the colours of the flags of the member-states. The blue stands for the sea, the sky and friendship. The emblem is formed of ten *padi* stalks, representing the ten member-states.

CARIBBEAN COMMUNITY AND COMMON MARKET

CARICOM is a regional organization, established in 1973 to promote unity, economic integration and co-operation between the small, insular countries of the Caribbean. It has a total of 14 members. The stripes of the flag represent the sky and the sea, and the yellow disc stands for the sun. The letters are the initials of the community.

ORGANIZATION OF THE ISLAMIC CONFERENCE

The main aim of the organization, founded in 1974, is to promote unity and to prevent foreign interference in the domestic affairs of the 35 member-states. The flag, in pan-Arab colours, was adopted in 1981. The green and the crescent symbolize Islam, and the inscription in the centre reads *Allah u Akbar* ("God is Great").

UNION OF THE ARAB MAGHREB

This was set up in 1989 to co-ordinate the communications and economic policies of its member-countries. The flag was adopted in 1990. The five stars represent the UAM members: Morocco, Mauritania, Algeria, Tunisia and Libya; the colours were taken from the flags of the member-countries.

COMMONWEALTH OF INDEPENDENT STATES

This was formed on the eve of the fall of the Soviet Union in 1991; the 12 member-states are all former Soviet republics. The flag was adopted on 19 January 1996 and the emblem symbolizes aspiration for an equal partnership, unity, peace and stability.

EUROPEAN UNION

The flag, originally adopted on 8 December 1955 by the Council of Europe, was taken over by the European Union on 29 May 1986. The blue symbolizes the sky, the 12 golden stars in a circle represent the union of Europe.

LA FRANCOPHONIE

This organization provides an institutional framework of official and private organizations and associations representing the interests of the French-speaking community, encompassing 47 countries. The emblem conveys the idea of bringing together and denotes the universal character of La Francophonie. The five parts of the ring symbolize the five continents where members of the community live (North America, Europe, Africa, Asia and Oceania).

COMMUNITY OF NATIONS OF THE PORTUGUESE LANGUAGE

The main aim of the CPLP (Comunidade dos Países de Língua Portuguesa) is to promote unity and co-operation. The flag, adopted on 17 July 1996, displays the historic colours of Portugal (blue and white) and a logo symbolizing the close ties among the seven member-states.

Regional and Local Flags

In the Middle Ages many European provinces were independent or semi-independent political entities, some of which have retained their original flags. But in central Europe provincial flags as such began to appear only in the 19th century, and most of them date from the second half of the 20th century. Throughout the world provincial flags fit into a general pattern that is particular to each country or has some features in common with other countries.

Some municipal flags, such as those of Genoa or Elbing, are among the oldest flags in the world but, like provincial flags, most were designed in the 20th century. With both provincial and municipal flags the principal factors influencing design are heraldry and the use of charges, whether these are armorial devices, Japanese *mons* or modern logos.

◆ **ABOVE** Flag display on a street in Lucerne. All civic and commune flags in Switzerland are in the form of a square armorial banner.

REGIONS AND PROVINCES

The first country to provide its provinces with flags (*Landesfarben*) was Prussia. In 1882 the government of Prussia approved the flags of Brandenburg, Hanover, East Prussia, Pomerania, Posen, Rhineland, Silesia, Westphalia, West Prussia and Hohenzollern. The provincial flag of

Saxony was approved in 1884, and that of Hessen-Nassau in 1892. All of these flags displayed horizontal stripes in livery colours, based on the arms approved or granted in 1881. The flag of Posen was changed in 1896 to show Prussian colours rather than Polish, and was changed

Alsace.

Auvergne.

Franche-Comté.

again in 1923 when Posen was united with West Prussia.

In many other European countries provincial flags are mostly heraldic banners. For example, the flags of the provinces of France and the counties of Norway are all armorial banners. Regional banners have been introduced in France during the last few decades but some, such as the flags of the duchies of Anjou and Maine or the kingdom of Burgundy, were already known in the Middle Ages. In contrast to the French armorial banners, which are quite complex, the flags of the Norwegian counties display single, simple heraldic figures. Many of them were proposed in 1930, but they were only officially adopted between the 1950s and 1989. The flags illustrated here were adopted in 1960 (Troms), 1965 (Nordland) and 1989 (Oppland). For a long time the flags of all nine provinces in Belgium were armorial banners. But now there are ten provinces,

FLAGS OF PRUSSIAN PROVINCES

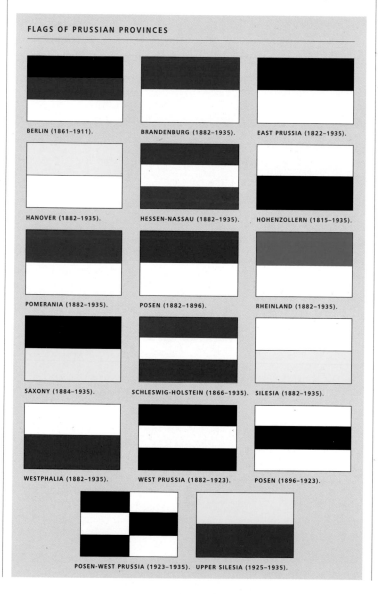

BERLIN (1861–1911).

BRANDENBURG (1882–1935).

EAST PRUSSIA (1822–1935).

HANOVER (1882–1935).

HESSEN-NASSAU (1882–1935).

HOHENZOLLERN (1815–1935).

POMERANIA (1882–1935).

POSEN (1882–1896).

RHEINLAND (1882–1935).

SAXONY (1884–1935).

SCHLESWIG-HOLSTEIN (1866–1935).

SILESIA (1882–1935).

WESTPHALIA (1882–1935).

WEST PRUSSIA (1882–1923).

POSEN (1896–1923).

POSEN-WEST PRUSSIA (1923–1935).

UPPER SILESIA (1925–1935).

PROVINCES OF NORWAY

Nordland.

Oppland.

Troms.

and some of the existing provinces have
adopted new flags. Heraldry has influenced
all the Belgian designs but the only
armorial banner is the flag of West
Flanders. Finland is the only country where
the provincial flags, which display the livery
colours, consist of very long pennants.

The flags of the Japanese prefectures are
modest yet very distinctive: their chief
characteristic is their uniformity of style.
Nearly all of them display a *mon* or logo in
the centre of a unicoloured field, often an

Thai Province of Nonthaburi

PROVINCES OF BELGIUM

Antwerp.

East Flanders.

West Flanders.

PENNANTS OF THE PROVINCES OF FINLAND

Uusimaa
Ruotsinkielinen Uusimaa
Varsinais-Suomi/
Ruotsinkielinen Pohjanmaa
Häme
Etelä-Pohjanmaa
Kainuu

Ahvenanmaa
Satakunta
Karjala

Savo
Keski-Pohjanmaa
Varsinais-Suomi

Pohjois-Pohjanmaa
Kymenlaakso
Lappi

Siniristi (koko Suomen
yleisviiri)
Keski-Suomi
Etelä-Karjala

PREFECTURES OF JAPAN

Hokkaido.

Toyama.

Tokio.

unusual colour such as dark brown, rust
brown, plum, lavender, violet or turquoise
green. These flags were adopted after World
War II, mostly in the 1960s. The colourful
provincial flags of Papua New Guinea,
adopted in 1978–1979, are very different.
Although they do not display traditional
heraldic figures, their appearance resembles
armorial banners. Most of the emblems
contain local birds or animals, insignias of
authority, leadership and bravery, or
artefacts used during ceremonies.

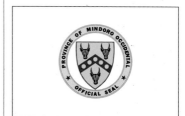

Province of Mindoro Occidental, Philippines

PROVINCES OF PAPUA NEW GUINEA

East New Britain.

Madang.

Simbu.

Provincial flags in other countries are either standardized, as in the Philippines and Thailand, or display common emblems or colours. Provincial flags in Morocco are square armorial banners with a *schwenkel*

PROVINCES OF MOROCCO

Casablanca.

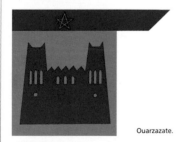

Ouarzazate.

in national colours, i.e. red with the green Seal of Solomon; the arms of the provinces were established in 1968. Provincial flags in Liberia have the national flag in the canton, while those in the Philippines display the seal of the province in the centre of a unicolour white, yellow or red field. The field of almost all the provincial flags in Venezuela is white and all of them are defaced with the coat of arms of the province. The only exception is the flag of Sucre, which is a diagonal bicolour of white and blue with 14 white stars in the lower hoist and the provincial coat of arms in the upper hoist. Thai provinces use the national flag defaced with the provincial emblem, all of which are circular. The flags of some Argentinian provinces display the national colours of light blue and white.

The most diversified provincial flags are those of the United States. Most consist of a plain field embossed with the state's seal and the symbol of authority, and in many the field is also charged with inscriptions such as the name of the state and the date of its foundation or

incorporation. There are a multitude of designs based on partitions of the field and displaying various emblems, and some of them are very innovative.

France has recently developed a series of flags that are unsuccessful from a vexillological perspective. The departments and regions, which as we have already seen have beautiful armorial banners, have also adopted white flags charged with logos in shapes and colours that are difficult to recognize from a distance. In most cases the logos are accompanied by long, illegible inscriptions. This, of course, means that it is difficult to recognize and distinguish between the flags when in use.

Nord-Pas-de-Calais. Typical example of new French regional and departmental flags.

UNITED STATES COUNTIES

Franklin (Illinois).

Santa Clara (California).

Sussex (New Jersey).

CIVIC FLAGS

In several European countries there is a general design for municipal flags. In Switzerland they are all square armorial banners. In Portugal they are square, gyronny and defaced with the full achievement of the civic arms. In Slovenia all the municipal flags have the proportions 1:3 and display the main heraldic figure from the coat of arms; the field is either plain or partitioned in one of ten different ways; seven have a square field at the hoist.

Slovakia is the only European country where the flags of all 135 cities and towns were established centrally by the Heraldry Commission of the Ministry of Internal Affairs. The flags are swallow-tailed, in proportions 2:3, and display the livery colours. 105 of the flags are composed solely of two to nine horizontal stripes, ten have fields charged with a saltire and ten are quartered. The flags of rural communities are triple swallow-tailed and also display the livery colours.

In Italy and Spain municipal flags are more diverse. Some designs, however, are more frequently used than others and are characteristic of the country, namely a

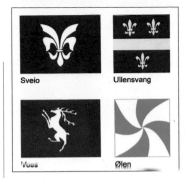

Sveio Ullensvang

Voss Ølen

vertical bicolour or a field charged with a cross in Italy and a plain field charged with a coat of arms in Spain. The use of a civic flag in the form of a gonfalon has survived in many Italian cities.

Municipal flags in Germany, Austria, the Czech Republic and Poland have several common characteristics. Most of them are horizontal bicolours or tricolours, they display livery colours and are often defaced with an armorial shield or the full achievement of arms. In West Germany just over 100 cities use the white-red bicolour, whereas the red-white bicolour has been adopted by more than 130 cities. Other bicolours are very popular there: blue-white (almost 90 cities), blue-yellow (65 cities), red-yellow (more than 60 cities) and black-

yellow (more than 50 cities). Much more inventive, distinctive and recognizable flags have been designed in recent years in Poland, the Czech Republic and the eastern part of Germany. The trend is to introduce more ingenious partitions of the field and to display some heraldic devices from the arms instead of the whole coat of arms. Ukrainian cities have begun to acquire municipal flags only in recent years and fewer than a quarter of the 1500 cities have their own flags. They are usually

Lviv.

Kovel.

Bari. Ancona (Italy).

◆ **ABOVE**
Typical examples of flags of the communes in Hordaland (Norway).

◆ **ABOVE RIGHT**
Two typical Ukrainian municipal flags.

◆ **LEFT**
Ceremonial flag of Rome, at the town hall.

◆ **RIGHT**
Polish municipal flags.

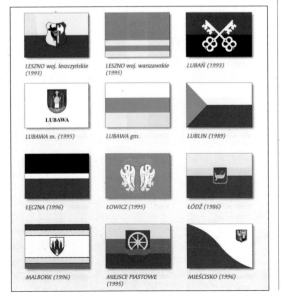

LESZNO woj. leszczyńskie (1993)

LESZNO woj. warszawskie (1995)

LUBAŃ (1993)

LUBAWA m. (1995)

LUBAWA gm.

LUBLIN (1989)

ŁĘCZNA (1996)

ŁOWICZ (1995)

ŁÓDŹ (1986)

MALBORK (1996)

MIEJSCE PIASTOWE (1995)

MIEŚCISKO (1996)

Millville (New Jersey).

Chicago (Illinois).

Kettering (Ohio).

Lubbock (Texas).

Memphis (Tennessee).

Milwaukee (Wisconsin).

Pittsburgh (Pennsylvania).

New York.

Amsterdam (Holland).

Barcelona (Spain).

Bergen (Norway).

Warsaw (Poland), Prague (Czech Republic).

City of London (United Kingdom).

Paris (France).

St Petersburg (Russia).

◆ ABOVE
(top two rows)
United States city flags;
(bottom two rows)
European city flags.

square, mostly charged with the civic coat of arms and with a decorative border. Official flags are mounted on staffs with a traverse bar.

Heraldry has very much influenced the municipal flags of Norway, Sweden, Great Britain, Finland, Belgium and the Netherlands. In the Netherlands almost all of more than 800 municipalities have their own flags. Over 20 per cent of them are composed only of several stripes (up to 13), in most cases horizontal, in some vertical or diagonal. The designs of the other flags are distinctive and very recognizable, with extensive use of livery colours and the main armorial figures instead of the full arms. Some of the most beautiful municipal flags have been created in South Africa since the 1960s. There are armorial banners, flags with the armorial shield or full achievement of arms, or flags displaying one or a few heraldic figures from the civic arms. Heraldry has also greatly influenced the design of municipal flags in many countries of the Commonwealth, mainly Canada and Australia. In the countries

of Latin America most municipal flags display the whole achievement of the civic coat of arms.

In the United States the most common design of a municipal flag is a plain field, in most cases blue, defaced with the civic seal. The second characteristic is an extensive use of lettering spelling out the city's name, the date of its foundation or incorporation, its locality in a state or county, and its nickname or motto. Some flags have graphic symbols with a written explanation

Flags of contrade in Siena.

underneath. As one vexillologist remarked, too many American flags are "literally littered by lettering". There is also a multitude of designs based on both traditional and unusual partitions of the field. The emblems are sometimes so intricate that they are imperceptible when the flag is flying; others are simple, modern and very distinctive. Many newer municipal flags as well as some older flags are excellent examples of ingenious flag design.

Some European cities have different flags for each district. The best known are the colourful flags of the *contrade* in Siena, in Italy, which date back to the beginning of the 13th century. Each *contrada* has its own mayor assisted by councillors. There have been 17 *contrade* since the end of the 17th century. Each *contrada* has its own colours, usually forming an intricate pattern, and an emblem that corresponds to the name of the district (for example, eagle, dragon, giraffe, owl, porcupine, unicorn, panther, and so on). These colours and emblems are used on the square flags which resemble armorial banners.

Flags of Peoples and Causes

Since time immemorial people have been eager to show their colours. In fact there was almost no mutiny, rebellion or defiance movement without its distinctive flag. Since the end of the first half of the 19th century, nations subjugated by world powers began to adopt their own flags. At first there were flags of nations living under the Austro-Hungarian, and then under Prussian or Russian rule. This trend continues, and today several dozen nations without statehood use their flags to denote either their identity or an aspiration to have their own state.

The 20th century witnessed the adoption of flags by political parties and fighters for freedom and independence. The flag of a political movement became the national

flag for the first time when the Nazi flag became Germany's national flag. The Nazis were also the first political movement to treat the flag as a political weapon. The use of flags during parades and rallies created an aura of might and invincibility; a tactic that was later copied by the Soviet Union and China.

Many current flags are closely associated with politics and the struggle for independence. Whether the flag belongs to the Albanians in Kosovo or the Palestinians, it manifests their defiance and aspirations.

◆ ABOVE
A demonstrator seen through an Albanian flag in Kosovo, March 1998.

◆ LEFT
Palestinian youths armed with a flag and stones approach Israeli soldiers on the West Bank, March 1988.

◆ RIGHT
Hoisting a giant flag to celebrate the anniversary of the liberation of Ho Chi Minh City, Vietnam.

NATIONS AND ETHNIC GROUPS

National flags for nations and ethnic or cultural entities without statehood first appeared in North America, where ethnic diversity is greatest. In the United States there are 558 federally recognized Native American nations and tribes. Twenty years ago very few had their own flags but there are currently about 180 tribal flags. Two acts passed by the Federal Government spurred the creation of flags: the United States Self-Determination and Education Assistance Act (1975) and the United States Indian Gaming Regulatory Act (1988) which allowed Native Americans to use gaming and tribal casinos as an economic resource.

The Arapahos in Wyoming adopted a flag during World War II and modified it in 1956. Red stands for the Arapahos, white for long life, black for happiness. Eleven Sioux tribes living in South Dakota have a

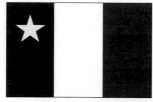

Acadians in Canada.

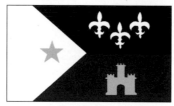

Acadians in Louisiana.

Arapaho.

Crow Tribe.

United Sioux Tribes.

common white flag. The number of tepees represents the number of tribes, and the arrowheads in the central emblem symbolize the four compass directions, the four seasons and the four natural elements. One of the most distinctive flags, designed in 1967, belongs to the Crows who live in Montana. The tepee symbolizes the home and its four poles represent the original treaty area agreed with the United States Government in 1868. They also stand for the four directions and the four seasons, i.e. for the limits or framework within which life takes place. The flag depicted here has the old seal; in the new one the white star and the stars of the Big Dipper (the Plough) constellation are omitted.

The flag of the Acadians who live in Canada, mainly in northern New Brunswick, was adopted in 1884. It is the French Tricolore with a yellow star, symbol of the Virgin Mary, and symbolizes the Acadians' fidelity to their origins and their faith. The flag of the Acadians in Louisiana was adopted in 1965 when they celebrated the 200th anniversary of their arrival there. It symbolizes their French origins (three fleurs-de-lis on blue) and the Spanish rule over Louisiana at the time of their migration (yellow castle on red). The yellow star symbolizes the Virgin Mary as Our

Lady of Assumption, their patroness, and also commemorates the Acadians' participation in the American Revolution.

African-Americans use the flag created in 1917 by the famous black activist Marcus Garvey for a new homeland for American blacks in Africa. Irish-Americans prefer to use a flag specially designed for them rather than the national flag of Ireland. It is based on the flags of the 1798 rebellion and the Irish motto *Erin go bragh*, meaning "Ireland for ever".

Many nations without statehood live in Europe. Some of them use flags that have become the flags of the regions. For their national flags the Basques, Catalonians and Galicians use the flags of autonomous communities in Spain, while the flags of the

Afro-Americans.

Irish-Americans.

Flamands and Wallons have become the flags of regions in Belgium. The Alsatians are descendants of Germanized peoples of Celtic origin, and those who are striving for a greater degree of autonomy use a red-white horizontal bicolour. The Breton flag displays an ermine canton and nine horizontal stripes. The ermine has been the arms of Brittany since the 12th century, the five black stripes represent the dioceses of the French language, and the four white stripes stand for the dioceses of the Breton language. The Cornish flag is black with the white cross of St Piran, patron saint of Cornwall, and dates back to the beginning of the 15th century.

One of the oldest national flags is a white flag with a Moor's head, an armorial banner of Corsica dating back to at least the 14th century. It is still used by those Corsicans who have never reconciled themselves to French rule over their island. The emblem of the Crimean Tatars, *tarak tamga*, appears in the upper hoist of the field of their flag which is light blue, the national colour common to all Turkic peoples. Although the Kashubians have lived for many

Crimea Tatars.

Gypsies.

centuries under German rule, they have preserved both their language and the consciousness that they are part of the Polish nation. Their flag displays the colours of the coat of arms of the duchy of Kashubia (black griffin on gold), not as a sign of separatism but to show their identity as an ethnic group with their own language, tradition and culture.

Normandy displays two flags: heraldic and modern. The armorial banner with two golden lions (one above the other) on a red field originated in the 12th century. The Scandinavian cross on the modern flag denotes that they are the descendants of people from Scandinavia (via the Vikings). Gypsies, or Romanies, were originally

nomadic people from India and by the end of the 16th century were living in many European countries. Their flag, not adopted until the 1970s, reflects the fact that the wheel enabled them to move freely on wide green plains under the blue sky. The wheel takes different shapes. One of the newest national flags is that adopted in 1986 by the Samis, or Lapps. For thousands of years these people lived in areas of northern Europe that now belong to Norway, Sweden, Finland and Russia. In 1956 they set up the Nordic Sami Conference, which in 1983 proclaimed the Land of Sami across international borders where they want to preserve their common language, history, traditions, culture and way of life.

Alsatians.

Bretons.

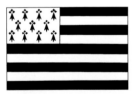
Cornish.

Corsicans.

Kashubians.

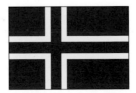
Normans.

Sami.

Scots.

The Scottish blue flag with a white St Andrew's cross is one of the oldest national flags in the world but the Scots prefer to use the Royal Banner of Scotland and some Scots living in the United States recognize the banner with the tressured lion as their national flag. The triskelion, an ancient emblem of Sicily known at least from the 4th century BC, is composed of three bare legs and the face of a Gorgon. It appears on the flag used by the Sicilians since 1990 as their unofficial regional flag. In 1848 the Sorbs adopted a flag in pan-Slavic colours: the blue stands for the sky, the red for love and the white for innocence. The Sorbs are the descendants of the Wends, a Slavic people who in the Middle Ages occupied large areas of the eastern part of Germany. Today they predominantly live in Lusatia.

Sicilians.

Sorbs.

In 1950 the Amboinese proclaimed an abortive independent state, the Republic of South Moluccas. Although it was suppressed by the Indonesian army, their use of the national flag manifested their will to be free. The red is the colour of their traditional dress and a symbol of courage; the blue is the sea and its riches; the white represents the beaches, a symbol of purity; the green represents the fertility of the land.

Amboinese

The flag of the Balkars, a Turkic people living in the Caucasus Mountains, was adopted in 1993 and displays the Turkic light blue and a silhouette of Mount Elbrus. The white stands for purity; the upper white stripe symbolizes the heavenly and spiritual attitude of the nation, and the lower stripe stands for their way of life.

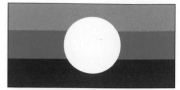
Shans.

Kurds.

Kachins.

Despite the numerous uprisings and promises by world powers that they will have their own state the Kurds, who live mainly in Iran, Iraq and Turkey, are the largest nation in the world still without statehood. Their flag displays the colours of the Iranian flag with a yellow sun in the centre. According to some sources there is also another Kurdish flag: a horizontal tricolour of red, yellow and green. There are several nationalities in Myanmar (formerly Burma) who are struggling to create separate states, among them the Arakans, Kachins, Karens, Mons and Shans. (The Arakans and the Mons in the past formed several kingdoms which existed until the 1700s.) The red and green of the Kachin flag stand for courage and the land respectively, and the crossed native swords represent the love of the homeland and the will to defend it. The flags of at least two liberation movements and parties are used by the people. The ochre in the Shan flag is the colour of the saffron robes of Buddhist monks, testifying that Buddhism

Balkars.

Australian Aborigines.

Kanaks.

is the national religion; the green stands for the land and for agriculture; the red denotes the Shans' bravery, and the white disc of the moon symbolizes their love of peace and their willingness to co-exist peacefully.

The Australian aborigines adopted their flag in 1971 but it was only decreed as their official flag in 1995. The black represents the aborigines, whose ancestors have lived in Australia for more than 40,000 years; the red stands for the earth and for the blood spilled by aboriginal people in defence of their land; and the yellow disc symbolizes the life-giving sun. The flag of the Kanaks, a people native to New Caledonia and striving for independence from France, was introduced in 1984. The colours are significant: the blue symbolizes the sky, perfection and sovereignty; the red stands for blood and the equality of all races; the green represents the land, and the yellow disc the sun. The silhouette of an ornamented spire symbolizes tradition.

RELIGIOUS FLAGS

Out of the main religions of the world only one has its own flag, which is used wherever the faithful congregate. It is the Buddhist flag, adopted in 1950 as the internationally recognized flag of all Buddhists of the world. Its five colours represent the five auras that emanated from the Buddha when he was in the Gem Chamber in the fourth week of his enlightenment. According to Buddhist belief, the blue is the colour of the Buddha's hair, the yellow stands for all impure secretions of the human body, the red for blood, the white for bones and for purity of words and deeds, and the orange for those parts of the body that are orange.

Of the many Christian denominations only a few have flags. There is no Catholic flag, but the yellow and white of the Holy See and the white and blue of the Virgin Mary are used to decorate churches at festivals. In the United States a fringed flag

of the Vatican City is used in Catholic churches and a fringed flag of the State of Israel in synagogues; there is also a Christian flag, designed in 1897 for use in Protestant churches. Some Protestant churches do have their own flags: the flag of the Episcopal Church is white with a red cross of St George and a blue canton with nine white crosses in saltire. Since 1938, Church of England churches have displayed a white flag with the red cross of St George and, in the canton, the arms of the see to which the particular church belongs.

In the United States and Great Britain there are church pennants to indicate that a ship's company is engaged in divine service. These date back to the Anglo-Dutch wars and were used to indicate a truce so that services could be performed at sea. In Catholic countries there is a multitude of banners designed to be carried in processions and displayed during

religious holidays. They are mostly pictorial in character, bearing painted or embroidered representations of the Virgin Mary, the Trinity or various saints.

The Muslims have mostly unicoloured flags, usually green, with religious inscriptions and simple emblems such as a crescent or the hand of Fatima. There are reports that in some countries the adherents of the Ismaili sect have a green flag with a red bend. The Sikhs, who live mainly in the Indian state of Punjab have their own flag, although some reports consider this an ethnic rather than a religious flag. It is a triangular saffron (orange) flag with a black traditional Sikh emblem consisting of a ring, two crossed daggers and a spear.

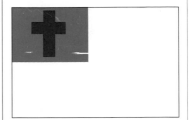

Christian flag.

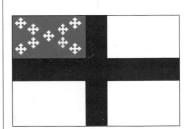

Episcopal church.

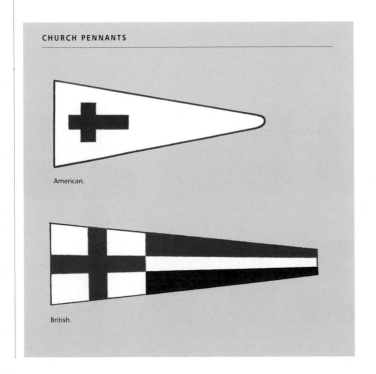

CHURCH PENNANTS

American.

British.

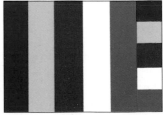

Buddhist flag.

FLAGS OF REVOLT AND DEFIANCE

Throughout the course of history social and political upheavals, rebellions and revolutions have always been carried out under a flag. Some of these flags influenced the design of national flags and a few eventually became national symbols; many more were carried by rebels who did not succeed in their struggle. Their emblems were either symbols familiar to the rebels or new symbols created to convey their ideas. For example, at the end of the 15th century German peasants rebelled under a white pennant with the emblem of a golden peasant shoe, *Bundschuh*, which in contrast with the boots worn by the nobility was a symbol of peasantry. The Bundschuh Rebellion flared up several times until 1525, when it was finally suppressed.

The taxation imposed by the British on the American colonists was met by defiance and led in 1765 to the foundation of the Sons of Liberty, a secret patriotic and radical society that was involved in the Boston Massacre (1770) and the Boston Tea Party (1773). Their flag displayed nine red and white stripes, symbolizing the nine colonies that participated in the Stamp Act Congress of 1765. The stripes in the national flag of the United States may well stem from this defiant flag.

Bundschuh pennant.

Polish peasants with their scythes upright played an important role in the Kosciuszko Insurrection of 1794. In the battles against Russsia they carried a red standard with the motto "Feeding and Defending" above weapons crossed behind a wheatsheaf. In the first half of the 19th century there were numerous kingdoms and principalities in the territory of modern-day Germany. Inspired by the French Revolution of 1830, the students from some of these German states began to agitate for unification. They adopted a flag with three horizontal stripes in the colours of the uniforms of the *Lützow Freikorps* and the inscription *Deutschlands Wiedergeburt* (Rebirth of Germany). Without the inscription, this flag became the national flag of Germany in 1848.

Australia's most famous rebellion was that of the miners of the Ballart goldfields in Victoria in 1854 against the imposition of licence fees. They raised a blue flag with a white cross bearing the five stars of the Southern Cross constellation. A few days

later the flag was raised again by a group of diggers at the Eureka Stockade, who took an oath, "We swear by the Southern Cross to stand truly by each other, and to fight to defend our rights and liberties". The stockade was overwhelmed by the police, but the Eureka flag became a symbol of independence and liberty, and inspired the design of the Australian national flag.

The newest addition to the flags of defiance and rebellion was that of the *Solidarnosc* (Solidarity) movement in Poland. In the first days of the famous strike at the Gdansk shipyard a young artist created a logo in which he spelt the name of the movement in such a way that the letters resembled people marching close together under the Polish national flag. Since then a white flag with this logo has been the symbol of opposition against communist rule, and in a free Poland remains the flag of the trades unions. In two known instances people in revolt did not need to adopt a new flag, it was enough to cut out the communist state emblem from the flag to show what they stood for. The first instance was during the Hungarian uprising of 1956, and in 1989 a flag with a hole in it was again carried in street battles in Romanian cities.

Flag of the Sons of Liberty.

Banner of Polish peasants participating in the Insurrection of 1794.

Flag carried by advocates of the unification of Germany in the Hambach Festival of 1832.

Flag of the Eureka Stockade, Australia (1854).

Flag of Solidarność (Solidarity) since 1980.

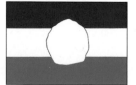
Flag of the Hungarian uprising (October to November 1956).

Flag of the Romanian uprising (1989).

Flag of the Federal Republic of Padania, an Italian state that does not officially exist.

FLAGS OF GUERRILLA MOVEMENTS

Vietkong.

Sandinistas.

Eritrean People's Liberation Front.

The Tigre Liberation Front.

The Western Somali Liberation Front.

SWAPO (South West African People's Organization).

MPLA (Movimento Popular da Libertação de Angola).

UNITA (União Nacional para a Independência Total de Angola).

FNLA (Frente Nacional para a Libertação de Angola).

FRELIMO (Frente da Libertação de Moçambique).

RENAMO (Resistencia Nacional Moçambicana).

Kurdistan Workers' Party.

In Italy a peaceful struggle to create a new state of Padania is led by the Northern League, formed in 1984. The Federal Republic of Padania was proclaimed on 15 September 1986 in Venice, but formally does not exist. Nevertheless the flag of Padania with a green "Sun of the Alps" is carried during demonstrations in favour of the new state.

Since the 1960s in various parts of the world, mainly in Africa and Asia, armed insurrections have aimed to achieve independence or to impose a communist regime. The best known are the communist guerrillas of Vietkong in Vietnam and the Sandinistas in Nicaragua. The struggle for independence in Angola was conducted by the MPLA (People's Movement for the Liberation of Angola); the FNLA (National Front of the Liberation of Angola) and the UNITA (National Union for the Total Independence of Angola). In Mozambique the struggle for independence has been conducted by two movements hostile to each other. The stronger one was the FRELIMO (Front for the Liberation of Mozambique) and its flag, adopted in 1962, displayed the pan-African colours. The other was the RENAMO (Mozambican National Resistance), which rejected both communist and fascist ideologies. The colours of their flag, adopted in 1977, symbolized the nation (blue) and the struggle for independence (red). The field was charged with RENAMO's seal. The Kurdistan Workers' Party is the main political and military force of Kurds fighting for their own state.

For more than a decade its flag has been seen in many cities of Europe during demonstrations for a free Kurdistan.

Two famous rebel flags are still in use. The "Jolly Roger" pirate flag is usually black with images such as a skull and crossbones, or skeletons with a scythe or hourglass. Some people claim that "Jolly Roger" is a corruption of the French *jolie rouge* and in fact the flags of pirates from the Barbary states were red. The jack of the Confederate Navy, used from 1863 to 1865, is also known as the rebel flag. It is still revered by some people and groups as a symbol of southern states' rights.

The Jolly Roger.

The rebel flag.

FLAGS IN POLITICS

Since late medieval times certain colours have had particular meanings. In Europe white was connected with purity and nobility. Red was originally the colour of empire and royalty but later became the colour of defiance, mutiny and revolution. The combination of red and black is used mainly by anarchosyndicalists. White was adopted by Francis I of France (reigned 1515–1547) and became increasingly popular as the colour of royalty, perceived as such since the 18th century, and today it is the main colour of royalist movements. Black is used on African flags to represent the country and the people. The colour can also have a dual symbolism, being the colour of mourning as well as defiance of law and order. Black flags were used by

Monarchists.

Anarchists.

Socialists.

Anarchosyndicalists.

FLAGS OF NATIONALIST MOVEMENTS

NSDAP 1920–1945. *Nationalsozialistische Deutsche Arbeitspartei.*

Flemish National Union.

Sudeten German Party.

Hlinka Guard.

Arrow Cross.

Rikshird.

Fronte della Gioventú.

Freie Arbeitspartei.

Afrikaner Resistance Movement.

Afrikaans Student Federation.

Yedinstvo, Russian National Unity.

National Bolshevik Party, Russia.

mutineers and pirates, and today they are the flags of anarchists and are often seen at protests. Many anarchists place a large white letter "A" in a ring on the black flag. Red flags were displayed as a sign of defiance as early as the 17th century. Sailors demanding better pay and working conditions hoisted them during mutinies at Portsmouth, England, in 1797 and at St Petersburg, Russia, in 1905. The same flag was used by the revolutionaries in France in 1830, 1848 and 1870, and since the Paris Commune (1871) it has been regarded as a socialist symbol, adopted in the 1920s by the communists in Russia. At the other end of the spectrum, it was also adopted by the Nazis in Germany.

The flag of the NSDAP (*Nationalsozialistische Deutsche Arbeitspartei*) was designed personally by Adolf Hitler, who combined the socialist red with two other colours of pre-war Germany. A white disc charged with a black swastika became the symbol used by foreign Nazis. The flag used by the Imperial Fascist League in Britain from 1933 to 1940 had the white disc and swastika in the centre of the Union Jack. The *Parti National Social Chrétien*, founded in Montreal, from 1933 to 1938 had a blue flag charged with a red swastika on the white disc. The flag of the NSDAP also served as a model for emblems adopted by nationalist movements in several countries, during Hitler's lifetime and afterwards. The flags shown opposite were used by the Flemish National Union in the Netherlands, the Sudeten German Party in Czechoslovakia, the Hlinka Guard in

Ethiopian Workers' Party.

Revolutionary Party of Benin.

People's Democratic Party of Afghanistan (1980–1992).

FRELIMO (since 1983).

Slovakia, the Arrow Cross in Hungary and the Rikshird in Norway; those currently in use belong to the Freie Arbeitspartei in Germany, two organizations in South Africa and two in Russia. One of the emblems, a black Celtic cross on a white disc, became the international symbol of young nationalists in several European countries. It is placed in the centre of a red field, as in the flag of the Italian *Fronte della Gioventú*.

The Soviet Union was a one-party state so the communists had no need to adopt a special flag. The red flag with a star and crossed hammer and sickle served all purposes and became a model for the flags of communist parties in many countries. Shown here are the flags of the Ethiopian

Workers' Party, FRELIMO (Mozambique) the Revolutionary Party of Benin, and the People's Democratic Party of Afghanistan in which the Soviet sickle has been replaced by a hoe. The fascist movements in Italy and Spain adopted emblems recalling the great past of their countries: the ancient Roman fasces and the yoke and arrows of the Catholic monarchs, respectively.

Many non-socialist political parties have flags displaying the national colours and often charged with the party initials. In Europe and the Middle East party flags display abstract emblems; in Africa and Asia they are charged with simple devices, mainly stylized animals such as an elephant or cockerel to symbolize strength, courage and perseverance.

Featured here is the flag of the National League for Democracy of Aung San Suu Kyi, who leads the struggle for democracy in Myanmar and was awarded the Nobel Peace Prize, one out of the hundreds of flags used by political parties in Asia. The flag combines elements of the flag of the Anti-Fascist Resistance Movement (red flag with a white star) with a peacock, the traditional Burmese emblem.

Socialist party of Belgium

National League for Democracy (Myanmar)

House and Private Flags

Most of these flags were introduced in the 19th century; indeed, many of them were introduced in the last half century. The most numerous are yacht and private flags, but there is a steadily growing number of house flags for shipping and trade companies, and all kinds of commercial firms. Tens of thousands of schools, universities, associations and clubs also have their own flags.

◆ **BELOW**
Flags of shipping companies of North and South America in 1933. Plate from *Lloyd Reederei-Flaggen der Welt-Handelsflotte*, Bremen.

COMMERCE AND BUSINESS

In the Middle Ages guilds and livery companies had their own banners, used during festivities and in battle. Some of the emblems they adopted, particularly in European countries, represented their trade or occupation: a pretzel represented the bakers; scissors, the tailors; a candle, the candle makers; a key or keys, the locksmiths; an anchor, the boatmen; and a boot or shoe, the shoemakers.

The first commercial flags were those of the English trading companies, used at the end of the 16th century. The most famous and long-lasting was the East India Company (established 1600), followed by its great rival the Dutch East India Company (established 1602). There was also the Dutch West India Company from 1621 to 1794, which established several

Smith's guild, Strasbourg (15th century).

colonies in the West Indies and Guiana. To distinguish them, their ensigns used national emblems, the English cross of St George and the Dutch horizontal tricolour. The Dutch ensigns differed only in their initials: "VOC" for the *Vereenigde Oostindische Compagnie* and "GWC" for the *Geoctroyeerde West Indische Compagnie*. A "C" above the "VOC" stood for

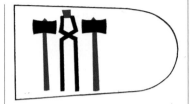

Smith's guild, Basel (15th century).

Capetown. The flags of the six chambers of the Dutch East India Company displayed stripes in different colours, with the initials "VOC" and an additional letter above it: "A" stood for Amsterdam; "D" for Delft; "E" for Enkhuizen; "H" for Hoorn; "M" for Middelburg, and "R" for Rotterdam. The Danish East India Company and the Spanish Philippine Company had their

Ensign of the British East India Company (c.1616–1707).

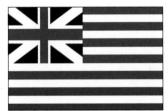

Ensign of the British East India Company (1707–1801).

Ensign of the British East India Company (1801–1873).

Ensign of the Dutch East India Company.

Ensign of the Dutch West India Company.

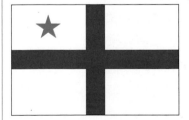

Italiana Trasporti Maritimi.

Black Star Line.

BP tanker company.

Midland Bank house flag.

P&O house flag.

Lufthansa house flag.

own flags based on the national flag. The modern house flags of trade and shipping companies originated at the end of the 18th century. These do not use national flags as a pattern, but sometimes adopt the national colours of their home countries. A rare exception was the flag of the Hudson's Bay Company, which from the 1820s used the British red ensign with the white letters "HBC" in the fly. Since the 19th century each shipping company has had its own house flag, which identifies the company to which a ship belongs. This flag or its emblem is also usually painted on the ship's funnel. The most common characteristics of house flags are simple partitions of the field, and extensive use of initials and simple emblems. One of the simplest yet most distinctive designs for a house flag is that of P&O (Peninsular and Oriental Steam Navigation Company), which became its logo and is used on its land vehicles.

The house flags of the shipping

companies inspired other commercial firms to adopt their own flags. Among the numerous airline flags, the most distinctive and attractive are (or were) those of Lufthansa, Air France, Sabena, BEA, Swissair and Qantas. Even better known are the flags of oil companies such as Shell, BP, Mobil, Texaco and Statoil, which are displayed at every filling station. Other examples of corporation flags are those of hotel chains (Hilton, Marriott, Sheraton and Holiday Inn), fast food franchises (McDonald's, Denny's and Burger King) and car

manufacturers (Volkswagen, Mercedes, Volvo, Chrysler, Ford and GM). Some corporations conduct business under different names and different flags (for example, Exxon in America, Esso in Europe). Others use flags in different colour variation, for example, Volkswagen uses a white flag with its logo in blue and a blue flag with the logo in white.

The best house flags have simple designs and distinctive features, making them easy to recognize. The general characteristic of a corporate flag is a plain-colour field with a simple corporate logo in the centre. If the logo is very simple, large and has a distinctive shape it is easy to identify from a distance, but unfortunately there is a multitude of flags with intricate emblems and a lot of lettering. As most of the fields are white, hundreds of house flags look alike and are unsuitable for outdoor use because they lack the important characteristic of distinctiveness.

Esso.

Getty oil company.

Statoil.

Volkswagen.

Sheraton.

Salvation Army.

World Scouting.

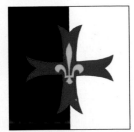

Federation of European Scouting.

Harvard University.

The Smithsonian Institute.

The College of Europe.

In the early 19th century many European countries set up clubs to promote national consciousness, for example gymnastic clubs in the Slavic countries run by Sokol (Falcon), students' corporations and choral clubs. Each of these clubs adopted its own flag or banner which was designed in the artistic spirit of the time. This trend became much stronger in the 20th century and flags and banners were adopted by youth, social and charitable organizations, scientific associations, clubs, schools, universities and even local fire brigades. Two examples of such flags are those of World Scouting and the Federation of European Scouting (FSE); both flags display the fleur-de-lis which is universally recognized as the scout symbol.

Universities and scientific institutions often adopt armorial banners. Their second choice is a unicoloured field defaced with a coat of arms, armorial shield or emblem. The armorial banners of Harvard University and the Smithsonian Institute show that not all flags in the United States display seals combined with lettering. The flag of the College of Europe bears a simple emblem composed of the letters "B" for Bruges, where the school is located, and "E" for Europe; the colours correspond to those of the flag of the European Union.

National colours are also displayed on the flags of vexillological associations. Just two elements – the national colours and the letter "V" (vexillology) – can create many different and distinctive designs. The

Italians made "V" part of their emblem, while the Bretons combined two "V"s (*Vannielouriezh Vreizh* – Breton Vexillological) in a saltire. In the Polish flag the partition line forms "W" for *weksylologia* (vexillology in Polish). The red saltire in the flag of the Belgian association recalls the cross of Burgundy and the yellow "V" stands for "vexillology". The Swiss vexillologists settled for an entirely different design, which resembles the Swiss military flags.

Flags of organizations are quite recent but personal flags have been in use since the beginning of the heraldic era. For example, in Great Britain the armorial banner of the Spencer family was established in 1476 and, before her marriage to Prince Charles, Lady

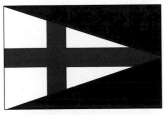

Flag Institute (Great Britain).

Vexilologický Klub (Czech Republic).

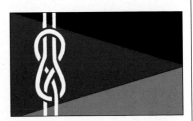

Deutsche Gesellschaft für Flaggenkunde (Germany).

FLAGS OF VEXILLOLOGICAL ASSOCIATIONS

Centro Italiano Studi Vessillologici (Italy).

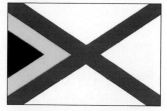

Societas Vexillologica Belgica (Belgium).

Polskie Towarzystwo Weksylologiczne (Poland).

North American Vexillological Association (USA and Canada).

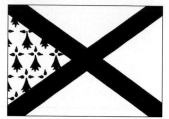

Kevarzhe Vannielouriezh Vreizh (Brittany).

Nederlandse Vereniging voor Vlaggenkunde (the Netherlands).

Diana Spencer was entitled to use it. The Spencer arms also appeared in the second and third quarters of the banner of Winston Churchill, who inherited them through the dukes of Marlborough. Many modern personal flags have also been designed by famous artists. In some countries there are festivities for hoisting private flags.

Two historic venues in Great Britain permanently display the armorial banners

Sociedad Española de Vexilología (Spain).

Société Suisse de Vexillologie (Switzerland).

♦ **LEFT**
Banners of the Knights Grand Cross of the Most Honourable Order of the Bath situated in the Henry VII chapel, Westminster Abbey in London.

♦ **RIGHT**
Banner of the Spencer family.

of the knights of two important orders. The banners of the Knights Grand Cross of the Most Honourable Order of the Bath are in Westminster Abbey in London. These are the Royal Banner, the Banner of the Prince of Wales, Great Master of the Order, and the banners of 33 knights. The armorial banners of the Knights of the Order of the Garter are displayed in the Choir of St George's Chapel in Windsor Castle.

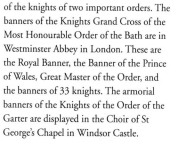

FLAGS IN SPORT

One of the oldest sports is shooting, and in the Middle Ages clubs for crossbowmen had their own flags. This tradition was taken over by rifle clubs, which still exist in many countries of Central Europe. In Great Britain cricket clubs, sailing clubs and rowing clubs have their own flags; the designs are usually based on simple field partitions and some display charges such as crosses, stars, three curved swords, a rampant horse, a rose, anchors or dolphins.

The first and best-known flag used in sport is that of the Olympic Games. It was designed in 1913 and was flown for the first time in public in Paris on the 20th anniversary of the foundation of the International Olympic Committee. The flag was first hoisted at the Olympics in Antwerp in 1920. The white stands for

Flag of Olympic Games.

peace and friendship between the competing nations, and the rings represent the five continents and denote the global character of the Olympic movement. During the opening ceremony a large Olympic flag is raised on a flagpole at the stadium and remains there during the Games. The athletes take the oath holding a corner of the Olympic flag and various forms of the flag are used during the opening and closing ceremonies. At the end of the 1992 Games in Barcelona the athletes held over their heads the largest Olympic flag ever made, 75 m (82 yd) wide and 105 m (115 yd) long.

The most widespread use of flags is by football (soccer) fans. After World War II many football clubs, mainly in communist countries, adopted flags but these were

rarely used and in most cases club regulations did not allow fans to use them. Instead the fans used homemade flags displaying the clubs' colours and even today in most countries flag manufacturers produce such flags, only rarely with the

club emblem. In the United States flag manufacturers produce different flags for the American football teams, with the clubs' colours in common. These flags all serve as a means of identification but in some sports special flags are used for marking and signalling. In many field games small unicoloured flags mark the corners or boundary line of the field and larger flags are used as markers to define the path in skiing events. In soccer the linesmen use two flags (red and yellow, one for each team) to signal to the referee a breach of the rules or that the ball has gone out of play. In car racing a black and white chequered flag is used to signal the end of the race.

Flag of the Redskins, Washington DC.

◆ LEFT
Banner of the Bavarian Rifle Association.

INDEX

NOTES

NOTES

NOTES

NOTES